T0168271

109 WAYS TO BEAT THE CASINOS!

GAMING EXPERTS TELL YOU HOW TO WIN!

Edited by
WALTER THOMASON

BONUS BOOKS, INC.
CHICAGO, ILLINOIS

04 03 02 01 00   5 4 3 2 1

ISBN 1-56625-144-3
Library Of Congress Control Number: 00-104514

Bonus Books, Inc.
160 East Illinois Street
Chicago, IL 60611

Printed in the United States of America

Table of Contents

PREFACE   v

INTRODUCTION   vii

PART I: TIPS FOR ALL GAMES   1
Casino "Edge"   1
Strategy   3
Odds and "Edges"   5
Money Management   7
Understanding the Rules   8
Understanding the Odds   9
Picking the Right Casino   11
"Comp" Programs   15
"Fun Books"   19
Gambling Tournaments   21
Tipping   23
Game Etiquette   24
PART II: TIPS FOR TRADITIONAL
TABLE GAMES   29
Baccarat   30
Blackjack   32
Blackjack Variations   50
Craps   52
"Live" Poker   63
Roulette   79

PART III: TIPS FOR MACHINE GAMES   83
    Slots   84
    Video Poker   89
PART IV: TIPS FOR OTHER GAMES   101
    Big 6 Wheel   102
    Bingo   102
    Caribbean Stud   104
    Keno   105
    Let It Ride   108
    Pai Gow Poker   108
    Red Dog   110
    Sic Bo   111
    Sports Book   113
    Three Card Poker   124
PART V: AUTHOR PROFILES   129
PART VI: ADDITIONAL RESOURCES   135

Preface

If you're like most people, you don't know how to gamble AND win. With the exponential growth in the popularity and availability of casino gambling in the last fifteen years, your ability to gamble and win has been further reduced because with nearly all of the games the casino is an odds-on favorite to win your money. In truth, you're more than likely to lose in spite of your skill level, because that's the way the games are designed; the gamble almost *always* favors the "house."

"So," you ask "Why bother to read a book about casino gaming?" Two reasons:

1. Short Run Results.

Casinos design games which favor them over the *long run*—millions of bets by millions of gamblers—and many players can experience short run victories that defy the built-in house advantage. The more you know about the games, the sweeter these victories can be.

2. "Best Play" Strategy.

Even in the long run, any player can reduce his losses at most every type of casino game, and at the same time increase his winnings when Lady Luck occasionally turns the tide in his favor. But to accomplish these results the player *must know* the best ways to play the games.

"But," you say, "I gamble for fun, and not very often, and don't want to spend the rest of my life learning how to improve my chances of winning. I've seen the books about casino gaming—hundreds of pages full of charts and statistics—and don't think learning all this stuff is worth the effort!"

You know what? You're right! Most recreational gamblers don't care about the hair-splitting finer points of gaming. They don't care *why* a certain strategy is superior to others; they don't care about the history of the games; they don't care about the personal experiences of the authors; they don't care about the charts or the formulas or the statistics.

Most casino gamblers are like you: They want a "short and sweet" path to successful play, and this is why we wrote this book. We'll tell you the best way to play every casino game—even the ones that are real tough to beat—in a few dozen words instead of a few thousand words. In most cases two minutes of reading will give you the condensed version of two hours of reading! These short and simple ways to win more (or lose less) will place you miles ahead of most of the other players, and give you an excellent chance of leaving the casino with some of *their* money in your pocket or purse. In this case, a little bit of knowledge can be a very beneficial thing!

Best of Luck!
Walter Thomason
April, 2000

Introduction

Estimates are that at least 80 million Americans participated in some form of legalized gambling last year, and that about half this number tried their hand at casino gaming. Attendance in casinos exceeded the total number of people that saw a live professional or college sporting event, or the total number of people that visited a major theme park. Las Vegas had more than 40 million visitors (average stay was two or more days,) Atlantic City had over 30 million visitors (mostly "day-trippers") and Mississippi casinos ran a close third in popularity, followed by at least a dozen states that have sanctioned the legality of casino gaming. Fact is, LOTS of people enjoy gambling in casinos.

The moral, ethical, or religious biases against this form of recreation have greatly diminished in recent years, due to better governmental regulation, a healthy economy, and more wide-spread availability of casino gaming. No mobsters, honest games, friendly casino personnel, fantastic facilities, great accommodations, super food, top-name entertainment, free drinks, and more!

Another fact is that most players don't have a reasonable chance of winning money in a casino! Why? Because they don't take the time to learn the basics!

This book is about basics—the *least* amount of knowledge that you should possess before you risk gambling in any casino—anywhere! The top names in the business of writing about casino gaming are contributors to this book. Their assignment was to provide *most* players with the *best* advice about how to play every game offered—in spite of the built-in advantage that casinos enjoy with practically every game offered.

Here's how it works: First, read the Table of Contents, then read *every word thereafter!* Each part of this book presents a variety of game-winning "tips" followed by an explanation of why and how the advice will improve your win percentage.

At the end of each Tip, you'll see two capitalized letters enclosed in brackets, like [WT]. These are the initials of the gaming expert who wrote the Tip. Writers who contributed to this book are:

[JG] = John Grochowski
[FR] = Fred Renzey
[FS] = Frank Scoblete
[AP] = Alene Paone
[HT] = Henry Tamburin
[WT] = Walter Thomason

Part One of this book gives you ways to improve your chances of winning before you enter a casino and make your first wager. Parts Two, Three, and Four tell you how to minimize your losses or maximize your wins, regardless of which game you choose to play. Parts Five and Six tell you about the experts that contributed to this book and how to purchase their publications, plus other books, audio and video tapes, internet web sites, and other publications that will improve your knowledge of casino gaming.

Incidentally, it's not our job to tell you how to risk your money in a casino. If you enjoy games like Roulette, Caribbean Stud, Keno, or Sic Bo—where the house has a very decided advantage over you—go ahead and play them! It *is* our job to tell you the *best* ways to play all of the games; ways that will help you lose less than the average player or win more than the average player. Casinos make their income from every game based upon the total amount of money wagered by the total number of players. The casino profit—their "edge"—varies from player to player. The information contained in this book tells you how to be *more skillful* than the average player, regardless of your game of choice.

Also, this book is not intended to be *all inclusive*. The casino gaming "tips" offered by our experts are only the tip of the iceberg to reaching long-term success. Our goal is to "wet your appetite" to learn more about how to successfully compete in the casino environment. While acting as the editor of this book, I picked up several new ways of improving my chances of winning—and I've been reading books and gambling in casinos for 30 years!

Follow the recommendations offered by the experts and your casino experience should be more enjoyable and, hopefully, more profitable!

Part I:
TIPS FOR ALL GAMES

Before you have a reasonable chance of competing against any opponent in any game, you must first learn the parameters of the playing field, the equipment required, the game rules, and the proper way to conduct yourself during the contest. Failure to learn the "basics" can take you out of the game before the competition commences.

These basic principles are especially important if you wish to be a successful competitor in the casinos, because your opponent is extremely well-versed in ways to make *you* the loser!

Even though this David and Goliath scenario will always exist when gamblers take on the casinos, we can have a good shot at defeating our gargantuan opponent if we enter the contest with the best resources at hand. This chapter addresses the basic tools we need to successfully compete against a very formidable foe.

CASINO "EDGE"

TIP #1: Understand that the casino has a built-in "edge" on every gaming option, and learn

1

how to reduce this edge through expert playing technique. [WT]

Before you place your first wager on any game of chance offered by any casino in any location, understand this one undeniable fact: The casino offers only those games which *insure* that they will win *more* money from players than they will *lose* to players. This built-in profit margin that allows casinos to be profitable business organizations is known as the casino "edge." This edge allows casino management to build huge establishments, offer lavish accommodations, great food, free entertainment, and other "perks" which attract us to their facilities. Without this advantage over the average gambler, they're wouldn't be a Las Vegas, or Atlantic City, or Biloxi, or Tunica, or Foxwoods, or any other profitable gaming location.

Consequently, if we wish to be successful casino gamblers we must first learn which games have the *lowest* casino edges; which games give us the best chances of winning. Then, we must learn how to play these games (or any games) *better* than the average player. Fact is, we can't force the casinos to play by rules which give us an even chance of winning. An "even" game—one that gives us a 50-50 chance of winning—would put every casino out of business in a very short period of time! It's their casino and their rules, and we must learn to deal with the built-in edge and try to overcome it as best we can! Throughout the remainder of this book, our experts explain the casino edge contained in every game, and offer ways to reduce the edge and improve your chances of winning. The knowledge you gain from reading this book, followed up with information in other casino gaming books, will elevate you above the "average" gambler, and allow you the opportunity to beat the casinos at their own games!

STRATEGY

TIP #2: Slow down the pace. [FS]

The one golden nugget of strategy that works for all games for just about all players is this: SLOW DOWN! What's your rush! Take it easy. Chill out!

Most people play casino games as if they are the human equivalent of four-wheel-drive vehicles driven by demented teenagers wearing backwards baseball caps. All casino gamblers—even those who have just turned 21—should rather think of themselves as delicate Desotos driven by fragile senior citizens. Your pace should be slow down, stop for a bit, wait for a minute, slow down again, stop, start slowly, rest for a bit, start slowly, and then take a break!

The casino has an advantage—an "edge"—ranging from about a half percent to over forty percent on their various games, and speed of play can only increase this edge in their favor. For example, mini-baccarat has one of the tiniest edges in the casino on two of its three bets: The "player" bet has a 1.36% edge, and the "bank" bet has a 1.17% edge. By contrast, roulette has one of the highest house edges, especially on the double-zero wheel—5.26%. The roulette bet is over 4.5 times worse than the mini-baccarat "bank" bet.

But will a player betting $10 a decision at roulette lose 4.5 times as much as the player betting $10 a decision at mini-baccarat? No. In fact, the roulette player is likely to lose less per hour than the mini-baccarat player even though he is facing a much higher house edge.

Here's how it works: Roulette at a crowded table can have 35 decisions per hour of play. So, a player puts $350 into action each hour ($10 X 35 = $350) and is expected to lose $18.41 ($350 X .0526% = $18.41). The mini-baccarat player can have as many as 160 decisions in an hour of play and be expected to lose $18.72 (160 decisions X $10 X .0117% = $18.72)—31 cents more! Even though I have compared a relatively slow game to a relatively fast game, you should see the point: SPEED can change a minor house edge into a major loss, just like speed can change a minor fender-bender into a major full-scale car crash.

Now that you know what speed can do, you can have your cake and eat it too (pardon my poetry)! Play a game with a low house edge and slow down! Play at crowded tables because the game automatically slows down, just as traffic slows down on crowded highways. Remember: Low house edge—slow pace. If your game is mini-baccarat, bet every other hand, or wait for trends or streaks or until the snow falls! The same pace works for roulette. Play at crowded tables, because the pace of any game slows down when more players are present. The mantra "SLOW DOWN!" fits just about every game, and should be applied by just about every gambler.

ODDS AND "EDGES"

TIP #3: The smart player should know the odds of all games he plays and he should know the edge, too. They go together like love and marriage, a horse and a carriage . . . Sing it, folks! [FS]

It's odd but true: Most casino players truly do not understand the odds they face in casino games of their choice. If they did, it would not be odd for them to immediately switch games to something a little more friendly to their wallets or purses.

The "odds" in a casino game are not the same thing as the "edge" in a casino game, but the odds and the edge are related. Take something simple, like roulette: There are 38 different pockets for the ball to fall into. Thus, on any given spin the ball will have a 1 in 38 chance of falling into any given pocket. The odds are 37 to 1—37 misses for every one hit! The "edge" is created when the casino pays 35 to 1 on a winning bet. Say you bet one dollar. Theoretically you'll win once for every 37 times you lose. So you lose $37 on your 37 losing spins. Unfortunately, the casino only pays you $35 for the one time you win. If the "odds" stay true to form, you can expect to lose $2 per 38 spins in the long run if you bet a dollar a spin, giving the house a 5.26% "edge."

Sometimes the casino doesn't have to short-change you on the payout to get an edge. In some games the odds determine the edge. For example, in craps the Pass Line wager will win 244 decisions for every 251 decisions it loses. The player loses seven more bets than he wins in 495 Pass Line decisions. That gives the house its edge of 1.414 percent on the pass line (495 divided into 7 = 1.414). Here the odds of 251 to 244 directly determine the edge.

But the odds show us an odd thing: that sometimes it is better for the player to play against a high house edge than to play a game where the player has an edge. For example, according to John Robison's article in *Chance and Circumstance* magazine (Summer 1999), the odds of hitting the Megabucks jackpot are 49,836,032 to one. The highest jackpot to date was approximately 27 million dollars, so no one has even come close to approaching a fair game on that machine (A "fair" game is defined as one where neither the house nor the player has the edge.) But let us say through some incredible run of bad luck (for the players) the jackpot has now grown to 50 million dollars. Technically, at this level of jackpot, the game is in a "positive-expectation" mode, since the machine is paying out more than the odds you face. In short, the player has a theoretical edge.

But in the real world, the player would be foolish to think he was going to come out of this on the plus end of a Megabucks equation—even when the game is giving back 50 million for the jackpot. Given a staggering bankroll of $10,000 with which to pump coins into the Megabucks machine, there's only an infinitesimal chance that a player will come out ahead in the long run. In fact, a person playing in a negative-expectation game such as roulette, which has a high house edge (5.26%) has a better chance of coming home with money in his pocket.

Here's the bottom line: The odds are not the be all and end all of gambling. But the odds help to determine the house edge either directly (as in the

Pass Line in craps) or indirectly (by the casino shortchanging on the payouts).

MONEY MANAGEMENT

TIP #4: Never exceed the amount that you've apportioned for each session of play, and quit play if you lose your session stake. [AP]

Most casino gamblers will lose in the long run because the casino almost always has an advantage. If you have $10,000 to gamble with, you can bet your money *fast!* Bet $1,000 or $2,000 increments. Most likely you'll "bust out" within a few minutes of play, regardless of the game you're playing.

Or you can choose to bet your money *slow,* and spread it out over time.

Money management is the art of stretching your money over time so that the potential long-run loss of your entire bankroll will last you through your casino experience. Follow my plan, and you'll still go home with money!

Using $10,000 as a guideline, how can we create a money-management plan that will stretch this cash until Armageddon? Divide and conquer, that's how!

Divide your money into "Trip" stakes, "Day" stakes, and "Session" stakes. If you know that you like to visit casinos five times a year for four days each trip, then do the following:

1. Divide five trips into $10,000. That equals $2,000 per trip.

2. Divide four days into $2,000. That equals $500 per day.

3. Divide four hours into $500. That equals $125 per hour.

When you've finished an hour of play, check your session stake. If you've profited, put it aside. The next session (the next hour of play) will utilize the *next* $125 in your hourly bankroll.

Conquer the casino by keeping profits when they occur. Win or lose, *never exceed your hourly bankroll!*

UNDERSTANDING THE RULES

TIP #5: Never purchase a mail order "get rich quick" gambling system. [HT]

Would you play golf or tennis for the first time without knowing the basic playing rules? Of course not! Yet when it comes to casino gambling, many players take the plunge without a clue about the basics of the games they play. The results are usually devastating to their wallet. Other, more timid players, shy away from what looks like a complicated game (like craps or baccarat) because they haven't taken the time to understand the playing rules. You will enjoy your casino experience and greatly improve your chances of winning if you take a little time to learn the basics.

Just about every casino provides players with a free "gaming guide" booklet, and many offer free lessons. This is a good way to learn "on the tables" without risking any money. You'll also pick up a few pointers on table etiquette, and specific rules that apply to the games offered in the casino where the lessons occur.

To learn something about the best playing strategies for your favorite casino game, read books like this one! Or read articles published in major gaming magazines, or purchase instructional audio or video tapes produced by knowledgeable writers. If you're computer-literate, you can purchase inexpensive software programs that will not only teach you the basic playing strategies, but will also alert you when you make a playing mistake. Addresses and web sites for reputable experts who will help improve your knowledge are included in the last chapter of this book.

And here's what you want to avoid:

TIP #6: Never ask for advice from other players. If you have to ask, you really shouldn't be playing!

To emphasize a previous point:

TIP #7: Expand your knowledge by taking advantage of the free or inexpensive advice offered by the publications, book distributors, and web sites listed in the "additional resources" chapter of this book. [HT]

UNDERSTANDING THE ODDS

TIP #8: When odds are expressed using the word "for," the casino keeps the initial bet, even

when the player wins! When odds are expressed using the word "to," the player retains the initial bet if he wins. [HT]

Casino gambling games are based on odds and probabilities. You don't have to be a mathematician, but you should have some understanding of "casino math" to help you select the best casino bets.

Let's keep it simple: The probability of a given event is a measure of the likelihood of its occurrence. Take roulette, for instance. The probability that the ball will land on number 7 on a typical 38 number wheel can be expressed as the ratio of 1 over 38 (1/38). The ratio represents the chance that the ball will land on the 7 compared to all of the possible numbers—38 of them. In casino gambling it is a common practice to refer to the "odds for something happening" and the "odds against something happening." In our roulette example, the odds against the 7 winning is 37 to 1, or you have 37 chances of losing for every chance to win.

Every casino bet has specific payout odds. If you bet $10 in blackjack and are dealt a blackjack hand, the dealer will pay you $15. Therefore, the payoff odds for a blackjack are 3 to 2 (you win $3 for every $2 bet.) Likewise if you bet $1 on #7 in roulette you will be paid $35 (35 to 1 payoff odds.) In some games the payoff odds are listed on the layout (as in craps) and in some games they are listed on the face of the machine (as in slots or video poker.)

Some casino bets have payoff odds of only 1 to 1—you win the amount that you bet—as in a winning hand in blackjack, a winning pass line bet in craps, or a winning bet on red in roulette.

Here's the catch: The words "to" and "for":

When you see the payoff expressed as "to" (like 35 to 1), it means that you that you win 35 chips, and get to keep the original chip that you bet. If the payoff is expressed as "30 for 1" it means that you receive 30 chips, but the casino keeps the original chip that you bet, which is the same thing as a bet with odds of "29 to 1." Casinos have been known to substitute the word "for" in place of the word "to" and most players never notice!

TIP #9: Learn the "basics" about odds, and only play games or make bets where the casino's "edge" is 1.5% or less. [HT]

The casino has the advantage on most every bet you make because it pays out *less* than the true odds of winning the bet. As you know, the odds of winning a roulette bet on #7 is 37 to 1. If the pay-off odds were the same, the casino would have no edge, and no potential profit, so they pay you 35 to 1 if you win and are assured of maintaining a 5.26% advantage, or "edge," over all players. The odds favor the casino . . . period! But players can enjoy the games and win money from time to time by playing those games that have low house "edges."

PICKING THE RIGHT CASINO

TIP #10: The games decide where you should play, and the amenities decide where you should stay. [FS]

I make a distinction between casinos I'll play in and casino/hotels I stay in. I've always said I'd play in a sewer if the games are good. By good I mean "beatable." If I could get the "edge" and maybe win some money, I didn't care what my surroundings looked or smelled like.

I have modified the previous statement somewhat because over the years I have played in too many damn sewers! Theatrical youthful boasts often end up on the cutting room floor of middle age. As a young man, I went for the money, all the money, and nothing but the money, so help me Midas. I'd gladly put my hand in a toilet (metaphorically speaking) if I could pull out some money.

You'll have to decide your temperament on this issue. Answer the following question before we proceed: Would you rather have someone give you a crisp, clean $5 bill, or would you rather put your hand in a cesspool and fish out a soggy $10 bill? At this stage in my life, you can have the cesspool, and I'll settle for the fiver.

But, I still believe that given a choice between two casinos whose waters you don't mind plunging your hand into, even if Casino "A" is slightly less attractive than Casino "B," if Casino "A" has the better games it gets my vote and my "action."

It's really a no-brainer: A video poker nut would be better off playing 9/6 jacks or better in a slightly less hospitable environment than he would be playing an 8/5 machine in a slightly nicer one. But if the slightly nicer place had a great slot club that made up for the lower level game, then that might tip the scales in its favor. The game—including the slot club and comping policies—decides. A craps player is better off playing in a casino with low table minimums and high limits on odds bets. A blackjack basic strategy player wants the casino with the best rules. A blackjack card counter wants the casino with the best deck penetration. But it's highly unlikely that all of these players would find their best game in the same casino. Again, the games decide.

But the games don't decide what casinos I'll stay at. If I'm on a trip to a casino town, I'm not staying in a rat hole just because the rat hole has a good blackjack or craps game. Life is too short to share your bed with vermin, eat with insects, or hobnob with hobos. I'd rather pay to stay at the Venetian than get a free room at Lucky Louie's, despite the fact that Louie has 27-inch televisions with triple X movies around the clock!

TIP #11: Stay and play where you feel most comfortable. [AP]

The right casino for me might not be the right casino for you. Like footwear and underwear, one size does not, never has, and never will, fit all! You have to select a casino based on your needs, wants, desires, and bankroll.

For example, if you desire to be comped to rooms and meals but you're a $10 blackjack player, you certainly would not benefit by playing at high-end casinos like Mirage or Bellagio. You aren't about to get many comps there. Conversely, if you don't mind paying a premium for a high-end room, don't mind buying your own meals, but love to play in posh surroundings, then by all means play at the aforementioned casinos. They have plenty of $5 and $10 blackjack games, and the surroundings are just what you want—elegant, beautiful.

However, if you are looking to maximize a rather short bankroll by playing in low-stakes games, then you'll want to play in "locals" places, or in low-end joints, where table minimums can be a dollar and sometimes less.

Picking the right casino to play in boils down to knowing yourself. What is your game of choice? What level can you afford or do you want to bet at? Do you want to play the "comp" game? What are your tastes? What type of environment are you seeking? Are you an advantage player looking to leave Las Vegas, Atlantic City, Mississippi, or another casino town with a profit, after deducting the costs of rooms, meals, and incidentals? If you are, the high-end casinos might be out of your economic reach. Are you a high roller looking to be given the royal treatment for the king's ransom you wagered? Then you definitely want to go to the pleasure palaces and stay out of the grind joints.

Of course, day-trippers aren't necessarily looking for the same thing as vacationers. Who cares what the rooms look like if you're never leaving the casino? For you, the type of crowd at the casino, the number and location of machines or table games, the friendliness or courteousness of the staff, and the ease of getting comps could be the determining factors in selecting a casino. If you find yourself becoming more and more dissatisfied with a place, then shop around!

Also, it is not unusual to "outgrow" certain casinos. When my husband, Frank Scoblete, and I first started gambling, we frequented casinos that we won't patronize now. Our needs and tastes have changed.

The selection process used to find the right casino is similar to that used to find the right marriage partner; not just any one is right for you—but when the right one comes along, you'll know!

COMP PROGRAMS

TIP #12: Sign up for the slot club in every casino you visit. [JG]

Slot clubs have become the casinos' prime marketing tool of our age. They're free to join—just sign up and you'll be issued a plastic card that you insert in "readers" when you play slots, video poker, or other electronic casino games. As you play, you'll build up points that you can redeem for cash, meals, merchandise, or casino services.

Beyond point redemption, you're likely to see your mailbox filling with offers of free or discounted rooms, bonus cash, invitations to special events, slot tournaments and more. When you join the club, you're entered into the casino's "data base." They know who you are, and they want to attract you back to their property.

This sometimes works even if you sign up and don't play! I signed up for a card at the Flamingo in Las Vegas, and received discount room invitations for the next three years, even though I never dropped so much as a nickel in a slot. I signed up at Caesars Palace to take part in a promotion in which $50 in play brought a $20 bonus. I played my $50 through on a video poker machine—hitting a full house along the way—took my profit on the game and the bonus, and left. Two years later, I'm still getting offers for room discounts and meals.

Offers become more generous when you actually play in the casinos. But just signing up can bring valuable returns.

TIP #13: Make sure your table play is rated if you wish to receive comps. [JG]

Casinos can't offer you comps if they don't know who you are. The primary goal of offering you free or discounted rooms, meals, or shows is to insure your loyalty. The casino wants your name and address in their computer so that it can follow up.

For slot players, that means joining slot clubs and using the club cards at the machines. For table players, it means *asking* that your play be rated.

At many casinos, table players can now use the same cards as slot players. Put your card on the table when you buy in or sit down at a different table, and the dealer will give it to a supervisor, who will rate your play.

Some casinos, especially older ones, keep table ratings separate from slot club ratings. Ask a floor supervisor to rate your play. He or she will start a ratings slip, and take your name and address. Later, you'll probably receive a table ratings card that you can just give to the pit boss when you sit down.

If you don't have your play rated, the pit boss and floor supervisor won't have a good handle on just how much you've played or how much you've wagered. Without this information, their ability to issue comps is limited.

16

TIP #14: For better comps, concentrate your play in a few favorite casinos. [JG]

Casino-hopping is a blast! Anytime I'm in Las Vegas, I like to walk several blocks on the Strip, take a stroll around downtown, and ride to a couple "locals joints."

But casino hoppers beware: Playing 15 minutes here and an hour there is not he best way to maximize your comps. Play a little at a lot of casinos and use your slot club card, and you're likely to receive a whole slew of room discount offers. If a $39 room is good enough for you, that's OK.

But for the really good stuff, like free rooms or free food and beverages, you're going to have to play longer in one casino. Casino marketers want to be fairly sure that they're going to get a good shot at your money before they invest too much in you.

Find a casino you like, with games you enjoy, good rules and pay tables, and concentrate most of your play there. You'll get more bang for your buck in comps.

TIP #15: Don't be afraid to ask a host for extra comps. [JG]

Let's say you've taken advantage of a slot club offer for a room discount. Near the end of your stay, you think you've played enough that your room should be free, and maybe meals you've charged to your room should be picked up, too.

Or maybe you've walked into a casino and, using your club card, played for a couple of hours. Now it's lunch time and you're wondering if you qualify for a comp buffet.

What do you do?

You could head for the slot club booth. But most slot club representatives aren't empowered to write your comp without deducting points. You may get your free room or meal, but it's going to cost you points that you otherwise could redeem for cash or other amenities.

Try asking the casino host instead. You can ask at the slot club booth, of if you're still playing for a while, you can ask a passing change person to send a host over. A host can write comps without deducting points. Then you can have your free lunch and your cash back too! If the host refuses, THEN it's time to think about redeeming points at the slot club booth!

TIP #16: Cash back is not always the best way to use slot club points. [JG]

The most popular way to redeem slot club points is for cash. That's understandable, but to automatically take the money and run without reading the slot club brochure for other redemption rewards could be a big mistake.

One casino I visit a few times a year offers $5 in cash back for every 20 slot club points, earned at $100 of play per point. It also offers a $20 meal voucher in its steak house for 40 points. These points would otherwise bring $10 in cash. If you want to eat in the steak house, it's much more advantageous to redeem for a meal voucher instead of for cash.

Other slot clubs offer merchandise worth more than the cash value of the points required. Of course, if you don't want the meal comp or don't like the merchandise, by all means take the cash. A bargain you don't want is no bargain. Just be aware of your options.

"FUN BOOKS"

TIP #17: Coupons can give you an edge over the house. [JG]

Fun books can give you a low cost sampling of what a casino has to offer. You might want to sample a free drink or a 2-for-1 buffet. But don't ignore the little "match play" vouchers contained in most fun books.

Such vouchers might offer a $2 payoff on a $1 bet, or $7 on a $5 bet. High rollers might turn their noses up at such propositions, but they're a bonanza for low rollers. They actually give the player a mathematical edge over the house.

I ran a little experiment for a newspaper article in 1993. I went casino hopping, playing match-play coupons and free coin vouchers. In one morning I made $36.75, with very little risk. I repeated the experiment in 1999, for a longer period of one morning and one afternoon. I played those little coupons into an $85 profit.

You'll lose your normal share of bets when you play with coupons, but the edge they give you is so large that if you always had coupons to play, you would be virtually guaranteed a profit. So, low rollers, heed this: Don't throw those Lucky Bucks away; they have real value.

TIP #18: Hit and run! Don't be afraid to make one bet and move on. [JG]

Casinos hope that when you stop to use a matchplay coupon, you'll stick around and play for a while. But you don't have to.

The instant your coupon is gone, your big edge over the house disappears. If you continue to play, you're bucking the normal house edge. If you want to continue playing, that's your decision. But if you want to keep the advantage, it's time to move on to the next fun book.

The only cost of moving on is the odd glare from a dealer or a shake of the head by a pit boss. Using a $7-for-$5 coupon at the old Sands in Las Vegas, I once drew a sardonic comment from a dealer. Nodding to me, she said to the other players at a blackjack table, "They come in here trying to win $2, and they bet $5 to do it. Can you believe it? Why do they do that?"

Of course, she was missing the point. I wasn't betting $5 to win $2. I was trying to win $7. If the casino gave those odds on every hand, it would go broke. If I had stuck around when the coupon was gone, I'd have had to bet $5 to try and win $5—just like everyone else at the table.

TIP #19: Look for funbook vouchers in freebie magazines. [JG]

Some casinos offer fun books for the asking at the promotions booth. At others, you don't even have to ask—it's difficult to walk past the Riviera at the north end of the strip without being handed a funbook voucher.

Other fun books are harder to come by, and

these include some of the best around. You can't just ask and receive; you need a voucher.

Where do you get the vouchers? Try the freebie magazines, such as *What's on?* and *Showbiz,* that are widely available in car rental agencies and hotel lobbies. A look through a couple of these magazines should send a low-rolling casino hopper on a mini-adventure.

GAMBLING TOURNAMENTS

TIP #20: In table game tournaments, knowing when to play it close to protect your bankroll by making small bets, and knowing when to let it all hang out and bet big are the two most important elements. [HT]

Playing in a gambling tournament is not the same thing as playing in a casino. With tournament play, you're not only competing against the house but also against your fellow players.

Although the rules may vary from one tournament to another, the basic concept is the same. All contestants start with the same playing bankroll. Your objective is to end up your playing session with more money than your fellow competitors. It doesn't make a difference whether you end up $5,000 ahead or $1. The player with the most cash wins.

In table games like blackjack, all contestants are assigned to a specific table and seat. Everyone at your table starts with the same bankroll. After a specific number of hands or set time limit, the player with the most money advances to the next round to play other winners. Eventually the field of contestants is whittled down to a final group of six or seven, who then play a championship round for the big prize.

Slot tournaments are different. Here players are given a specific playing bankroll or machine credits. After a specified number of handle pulls or at the end of a specific time period the player with the most credits (or winnings) advances to the next round.

The fascination of tournaments is that contestants are competing against each other. Therefore you must watch not only the status of your own bankroll but also that of your fellow players.

How you bet in table game tournaments is the most important factor to improving your chances of winning. Betting strategies employed by your competitors, whether you are ahead or behind the leader, and whether you bet first or last are factors that must be considered.

TIP #21: In slot tournaments, *speed* is the most important element, since your goal should be to hit the spin button very rapidly in order to maximize the number of spins possible within the allotted time limit. [HT]

TIP #22: Shop around, and only play tournaments where 100% of the entrance fees are returned in the form of prize money. [HT]

No matter what tournament you decide to try, always check whether the tournament returns all of the fees in the form of prize money. Most do, and then throw in discounted rooms, free welcome buffets, and other goodies to tournament players. Obviously the casino's motivation is to attract you to their establishment for the tournament, and win lots of money from you during your normal casino play!

TIPPING

TIP #23: Give generously to those who provide good service to you! [FS]

Many service industry jobs such as waiter, waitress, barber, beautician, bellhop, and maid are structured in such a way that tips from patrons constitute the major portion of a living wage. When I worked as a waiter during my college days many eons ago, I received 90 cents an hour as a salary. If I didn't get tips, I'd have difficulty paying my rent and food bills. In a very real way I was working for the people who paid my bills—the folks who ate at the restaurant—more so than for the folks who owned the restaurant, whose salary basically paid my transportation costs to and from work. I had to hustle. I had to give good service. I had to be good to every single customer or I would suffer the consequences.

In casino-hotels across the land, you'll find that many workers are in the "I need tips to survive" category. If the service is good, then the following are guidelines on what to tip the various service workers:

1. Valet Parkers: $2 to $3 when they bring your car.

2. Bellhops: $1 to $2 per piece of luggage.

3. Waiters and Waitresses: 20% of pre-tax bill.

4. Dealers: No hard and fast rule as to the amount. However, a few tips every hour that are approximately 10 to 20% of an average bet is not a bad rule-of-thumb. Note: When tipping dealers, put your tip on top of your bet so that the comp-raters include it in your rating!

5. Slot Attendants: If you win a big, hand-paid jackpot, it is customary to give $20 to $100 if the jackpot is rather large.

6. Maids: The most under tipped workers in the world! Give at least $3 to $5 a day.

GAME ETIQUETTE

TIP #24: Knowing the proper etiquette will save you time and personal embarrassment. When in doubt about the procedures of a given game, ask the dealer or floor person for help. [AP]

When in Rome, do as the Romans do. When in Ceasars Palace or any other gambling hall in America, you must do as the gamblers do—which is obey the rules of gaming etiquette that have been developed over the years.

1. When you buy into a game, never hand your money directly to a dealer. Put it on the table. The dealer will take it and convert your cash to chips. In craps games, wait until the dice are in the middle of the table. Do not cash in when the shooter is about to roll!

2. In card games where the cards are dealt

face up, you cannot touch them. You must make all your decisions based on hand signals. If you want a card, point your index figure at your cards for a "yes." If you don't want a card, wave your hand over the cards for a "no."

3. If you want to split or double-down in face-up blackjack games, you simply put up the extra bet and say "split" or "double." The dealer will move the cards and chips to the proper positions.

4. In card games where the cards are dealt face down, you are allowed to touch the cards. If you want a hit at blackjack, you "scratch" your cards along the felt. If you want to stand, you slide your cards—face down—under your bet. If you want to double-down or split in face-down blackjack games, turn your cards face up, and put up the extra money. On a split, you actually move the pair away from each other and put up the extra bet.

5. When you're the shooter at craps, both dice must hit the back wall. Also, when not shooting, never dangle your hands over the table where the dice can hit them.

6. When you are cashing out of a game, put your chips in a pile and say, "color me up." The dealer will take your smaller denomination chips and exchange them for larger denomination chips.

7. If you wish to exchange large denomination chips for smaller denomination chips, place the chips on the table (not in the betting box!) and say, "change please."

8. Clean up after yourself at the slot machines. Don't leave wrappers inside the coin trays or cigarettes outside the ash trays.

9. Don't give other players unsolicited advice on how to play.

TIP #25: Negative thoughts, expressions, or opinions never helped anyone win money in a casino! [WT]

A final word about etiquette: Don't ruin the game for other players by telling them how much you're losing, how unfair the rules are, how stupidly they played their last hand, how wrong they were to raise their last bet, etc., etc. Each player chooses to gamble—risk his money—as he sees fit. It's his business, not yours. If you disagree with the actions of another player, move on to another game and keep your opinions to yourself! If you can't offer a word of praise or encouragement to your fellow players, keep your mouth shut!

TIP #26: Don't expect to lose! [WT]

One final tip before we move on . . . Some of the most common statements I hear from fellow players, regardless of the game, is "Well, I expect to lose." "The casino wouldn't be here if I had any chance of winning." "It's my hobby, and I expect to pay for it." "There's no way to beat these guys. As long as they treat me nice, I don't mind losing."

In my opinion, all of these rationalizations are "BS"—not the slang word for what exits from a bull's rear end, but a term that I think best expresses why most players lose: BEFORE STRATEGY.

Most players that are consistent losers are poor strategists. They don't understand the initial odds against them, and they don't take the time to learn how to combat these odds. They expect to lose, and, by golly, they do! They allow themselves to be victims of a self-fulfilling prophesy, and aren't disappointed when the worst scenario occurs.

Personally, I HATE TO LOSE, and spend a lot of time learning how to best compete against the odds facing me. You should do the same thing!

So there you have it . . . much of the basic knowledge that you should have before you set foot in a casino. The following parts of this book go into specific details that will help reduce the casino's advantage over you. From this point on, we get into the nitty-gritty; we talk about money! Your money, the casino's money, and what you can do to swing the odds of winning in your favor.

Part II:
TIPS FOR TRADITIONAL TABLE GAMES

In spite of the current popularity of slot machines and video poker, lots of table games have withstood the test of time and remain the first choice of many casino gamblers. All of the traditional favorites are games that originated hundreds, perhaps thousands of years ago. Two of them (Roulette and Baccarat) are European transplants, and three of them (Blackjack, Craps, and Live Poker) are "Americanized" versions of games dating back to the great dynasties of China and the Pharaohs of Egypt. Perhaps all of them have appealed to gamblers at one time or another, which accounts for their longevity.

Other than their historical heritage and long-standing popularity, these games have little in common, and each has its own unique characteristics—most of which cause most of us to lose more money than we win!

In this chapter our experts will tell you the *best ways* to play these games.

BACCARAT

TIP #27: Play baccarat in casinos that only charge 4% on the "bank" hand. [HT]

Baccarat is one of the simplest and best casino games to play. It is often played by high rollers (known as "whales") in a plush area of the casino known as the "baccarat pit." But you don't need a big bankroll to get in on the action. A lower stakes games, known as mini-baccarat, is available on the main casino floor. Whichever game you choose, the rules are predetermined, and players can't alter the outcome of play. Incidently, the last syllable in baccarat is pronounced, "ra*h*", not "ra*t*."

What many players don't realize is that some casinos charge a higher commission on the "bank bet" than others. The normal commission for betting on Banker is 5%, but some casinos—those in competitive environments—have reduced this "vig" to 4%.

TIP#28: Don't make the tie bet in baccarat. [JG]

Baccarat is one of the easiest games in the casino, in spite of its apparent complexity. It's a simple guessing game: Which hand will total closer to 9—Banker or Player? There are no strategies to memorize, and all Hit/Stand decisions are made according to pre-set rules which can't be altered by either the player or the dealer. The player's only decision is which bet to make: Player, Banker, or Tie.

There is one pitfall. Betting on ties will drain

your bankroll fast. It's a tempting proposition. Bets on Banker or Player pay only even money, while the Tie bet pays 8-1. Problem is, ties don't occur once for every 9 hands, which would make an 8-1 payoff an even bet. They don't even pop up once per 10 hands, which would give the house a horrendous edge of 10%. Ties happen only about every 10.5 hands, and the house has an edge of 14.4%!

For every $100 you bet on ties, you can expect an average of $14.40 to vanish into the house's tiller. There's a word for bets like this: Yuck!

TIP #29: Banker is your best baccarat bet. Pay the commission. [JG]

Banker and Player in baccarat both rank among the best bets in the casino. The house edge on Banker is only 1.17%, while on Player it's only 1.36%.

In fact, the Banker bet is unusual because it's one of the few that actually wins more often than it loses. How can the house afford to offer such a bet? By charging a 5% commission on winning wagers.

That commission scares off some newcomers. Why would you want to make a bet that forces you to give the house a share of your winnings? Answer: Because even with the commission, the house edge is one of the lowest of any game offered.

Player is a good bet too, and there's nothing wrong from switching from one to another, or riding streaks. But the bottom line is that the smallest house edge at the table is on Banker.

TIP #30: Slow down, and play big bac instead of mini-bac. [JG]

Mini-baccarat, played on a blackjack-size table, has the same rules as regular baccarat, which is played on a 14-player table. But big baccarat, traditionally a high-roller's game, moves at a more stately pace than mini-bac. Many casinos retain some ceremony at big bac, passing the shoe and having players deal the cards. At mini-baccarat the games moves more rapidly, with dealers pushing out cards as quickly as they can.

In any game, speed compounds the house edge; The faster the game, the higher your expected loss per hour. You'll usually find higher minimum bets at big baccarat tables, but if you're going to bet enough to beat the minimum anyway, your money will go farther at the big, slower table.

BLACKJACK

TIP #31: Blackjack is the best casino table game because it can be beat by skillful players. [HT]

Why play blackjack? Of all the casino games, why bet on blackjack? What makes it different than every other casino table game?

For one, the odds in blackjack are not constant. They keep changing from one hand to the next, depending on the cards that have been played. For example, if four Aces have been dealt from a single deck of cards, the chances of getting a blackjack on the next round is zero. The cards, if you wish, have a memory. That's not the case with craps, roulette, amd other casino games where the odds stay the same from one roll or spin to the next. The dice and the wheel have no memory. The net result is that blackjack is a game of SKILL, not just luck.

Another factor that separates blackjack from other games is that players must make a playing decision after they make their initial bet. Their decision may have a great influence on whether they win or lose a hand.

Blackjack is also the most studied and analyzed casino game. Computer derived basic playing strategies have been developed that can significantly decrease the normal casino advantage. In fact, it's possible for the average player to lower the casino's edge by learning how to count cards.

So why play blackjack? Because it is a "beatable" game, and it gives the skilled player the best shot at winning.

TIP#32: Seek out blackjack tables with the most favorable rules. [JG]

Not all blackjack games are created equal. There's a wide range of rule variations, some good for the player, and some designed to do nothing but pad the house advantage.

Among the rules that are good for the player: Dealer stands on all 17s; player may double-down on any first two cards; player may double down after splitting pairs; player may resplit Aces; player may surrender (after his first two cards, the player may surrender half his bet in exchange for not having to play out the hand.)

Among the rules that are bad for the player: Dealer hits soft 17, double-downs are restricted to

9, 10, or 11; player may not double after splitting pairs; player may not resplit pairs; player may not resplit Aces.

Do you see a pattern here? Player options—rules that give the player the most room to make decisions—are good, provided the player knows how to use them. Rules that restrict player decisions are bad.

The number of decks also enters the picture. If all other rules are equal, fewer decks are better. The house edge is lowest with a single deck, makes its biggest jump in switching from one deck to two, and increases by lesser amounts with each deck added to the shoe.

That doesn't mean the game with fewer decks is the one we always want to play. The overall effect of the rules must be considered. In my neck of the woods, I can play a six-deck game in which the dealer stands on all 17s, I may double on any first two cards, double after splits, split and resplit up to a total of four hands, and may resplit Aces—all good rules except for the six decks. Another nearby casino offers two-deck blackjack, but restricts double-downs to two-card totals of 9, 10, or 11, does not allow me to double after splits and does not allow resplitting of pairs, let alone Aces.

Guess what? The six-deck game is a much better game. That's where I play.

TIP #33: Don't guess! Learn basic strategy. [JG]

Blackjack is not a game of hunches or "feeling lucky." Blackjack is a game of percentages; the most intensely studied of casino games. And one thing card counters, progression bettors, or anyone who plays intelligently can agree on is that the place to start is with Basic Strategy.

Using Basic Strategy to decide when to hit or stand, or when to split or double down, takes the guesswork out of blackjack. There's no hemming or hawing over your 16s when the dealer has a 10 face up, no drawled out, "I don't think she has it this time," while standing on a hand that can't win unless the dealer busts.

Basic Strategy already takes into account that the dealer, starting with a 10 up, is going to make 17 or better without busting 78% of the time, and you'd best hit that 16 to give yourself a fighting chance. There's no guarantee that you'll win, but in the long run you'll do better if you follow the Basic Strategy plan on every hand.

In books solely devoted to blackjack, you'll find the Basic Strategy tables covering every possible situation—tables you can use to drill yourself as you practice at home. But for the time being, let's take a look at a down and dirty, quick version of Basic Strategy, one that misses a few of the finer points but still will take the house edge down under 1% at most blackjack tables:

1. Always stand on 17 through 21, except always hit soft 17.

2. Hit 12 through 16 when the dealer shows a 7 or better.

3. Stand on 12 through 16 when the dealer shows a 2,3,4,5, or 6.

4. Always split Aces and 8s.

5. Double down on 10 or 11 unless the dealer shows a 10 or Ace.

6. Hit any total of 9 or less.

This strategy isn't perfect. A complete version of Basic Strategy would show that we hit 12 when the dealer shows a 2 or 3, or that we double on 11—even against a 10. It glosses over a bunch of opportunities to split or double down. But as an easy, conservative jumping-off point, this abbreviated version of Basic Strategy takes much of the guesswork out of the game and makes you better than the majority of other players.

TIP #34: Unless you're counting cards, never take insurance—even if you have a blackjack. [JG]

Beware of bets advertised in big letters taking a lot of space on the table layout—Insurance, for example.

Whenever the dealer has an Ace face up, he'll offer you insurance. You may then "insure" your hand by making a bet half the size of your original wager. If the dealer then has a 10-value card down to complete a Blackjack, your insurance bet is paid 2 to 1.

Say you bet $10, and you're dealt a 20. The dealer has an Ace up, so you make a $5 insurance bet. The dealer turns up a 10, so you lose your original $10 bet, but you're paid $10 on your insurance bet. Thanks to insurance, you're all even.

If you have a two-card 21, you don't even have to put up the second wager at most casinos. Just call out, "Even money." You forfeit the 3-2 bonus payoff on blackjack, but are paid even money on your original bet, even if the dealer also has blackjack. For your $10 bet, you get $10 in winnings, regardless of the dealer's final hand.

Sound like a good deal? Only if you don't think about it too hard.

What if the dealer doesn't have a 10 down? Those 3-2 payoffs you don't collect on Blackjacks add up, and so do those $5 insurance bets on any other hand. That's what happens 69.2% of the time—the dealer doesn't have Blackjack, and you're throwing your money away.

Insurance insures nothing. It is a separate bet that the dealer has Blackjack. At a 2-1 payoff, that would be an even proposition if one-third of the cards in the deck had values of 10. But only 30.8% of the cards in the deck have values of 10, and that makes insurance a losing proposition for the player.

The only players who should take insurance are card counters who know that an excess of small cards have been played and that a third or more of the remaining cards have values of 10. For everyone else, taking insurance is just giving an extra edge to the casino.

TIP #35: Always splits aces or eights; never split 5s or 10s. Follow up with the correct splitting strategy. [JG]

The decision to split pairs often depends on what card the dealer has face up. But for some pairs, there is no ambiguity. The Basic Strategy player *always* splits Aces and 8s, and *never* splits 5s or 10s.

Sometimes splitting is an offensive measure and sometimes it's defensive. Against a 6, we'll split Aces or 8s because we're hoping to win both hands, whether through a dealer bust or through a good draw on our cards. Against a dealer's 10, we split Aces hoping we'll pull at least one high card that will give us a split decision, and we split 8s because hard 16 is such a terrible start. Splitting doesn't always put us in a winning situation, but we'll lose less money in the long run with two hands starting with 8 than with one hand starting with 16.

Starting with 5s or 10s puts us at the other end of the spectrum. If we split 10s, we're breaking up a hand that can lose only if the dealer pulls a 21. If the dealer has a 5 or 6 up, we'll win so much more often if we start with 20 than with two hands starting with 10, thus we're giving away some of our profit if we split the pair.

Splitting 5s is even worse. That breaks up one of our prime building blocks—a 10—in favor of two weak ones in two hands of 5. Rather than getting extra money on the table by splitting the pair, treat the pair of 5s as a 10, and double down whenever the dealer shows a 2 through 9.

TIP #36: Know when to double down. [JG]

The house advantage in blackjack comes from one simple fact: We players have the first opportunity to go bust. When we bust, we lose—even if the dealer also goes bust.

If we play the same strategy as the dealer, always hitting 16 or less, and always standing on 17 or more, the house edge would be about 8%, equal to the 8% of hands on which player and dealer would bust together.

The casino gives us part of that edge back by paying 3-2 on Blackjack, and most of the rest back by allowing us to decide when to hit, stand, split pairs, or double down.

We can double down after seeing our first two cards by making a second wager equal to our first. Then we get just one more card.

It's up to us to know when that's an opportunity and not a trap. We want to put more money on the table when the situation is in our favor, but we don't want to throw extra money away when the house has the edge.

To cut the house edge even lower than the "down and dirty" basic strategy previously detailed, take advantage of these opportunities: Double down on 11 when the dealer has anything but an Ace; on 10 when the dealer has anything but 10 or Ace, and on 9 when the dealer shows 3 through 6. If you're playing single-deck, we should double 11 vs. a dealer's Ace, 9 vs. a dealer's 2, and 8 vs. a dealer's 5 or 6.

We also want to double on some "soft" hands—hands in which an Ace is being counted as 11, and cannot be busted in a one-card draw, since the Ace could revert to being counted as 1. For the following hands: Double soft 13 or 14 against 5 or 6; double soft 15 or 16 against 4, 5, or 6; double soft 17 or 18 against 3 through 6. In single-deck, also double soft 13 or 14 against a 4, and soft 17 against a 2. These playing decisions will maximize your opportunities to win, and reduce the casino's opportunities to drain your bankroll.

TIP #37: Purchase a blackjack book written by a knowledgeable author (see the additional resources chapter of this book), and learn basic strategy.

TIP #38: Learn a simple one-level card counting strategy that you can use to vary your bet size and your playing strategy. [HT]

The best "house banked" casino table game—if you are serious about winning—is blackjack. By skillfully playing your hands it's possible to reduce the casino's edge to less than 1%, and with advanced card counting strategies you can actually turn the tables on the casino and have the edge over them.

Once you've learned to select the best playing rules and have mastered Basic Strategy, the mathematically proven betting strategy that will swing the edge in your favor is called *card counting.* This strategy allows you to keep track of the ratio of high and low value cards remaining in the deck or shoe as the game progresses. It's been proven many times over through millions and millions of computer studies that whenever the remaining undealt cards contain more high-value cards (10s, picture cards, and Aces) compared to low-value cards (2s through 6s) the edge shifts in the player's favor.

Likewise, when the reverse occurs and the remaining cards contain an abundance of low-value cards vs. high value cards, the edge swings in favor of the casino. Card counters know (by counting) when the edge swings in their favor and that is when they bet more money. Likewise, they bet less when the edge is with the casino.

By varying the bet size based upon the count, it is possible to gain the long-term mathematical advantage—for a short period of time. Advanced card counters may also vary Basic Strategy, based on the count.

TIP #39: Always hit 16 against a 7! [FR]

There's a common mistake made by experienced blackjack players, and it's a *big* one! Many players will hit 16 against a face card all day long, but when they've got a big bet riding or have built up a hand like *4/3/5/3/Ace,* they'll stand against a dealer's *7!* Not only is this wrong—their thinking is all backwards! The player may have been correct to stand with a long, drawn-out *16* against a *10* up, but *never* against a *7.* Why? Follow along with me while I explain *the numbers within the numbers.*

When the dealer has a 10 up and you get the chance to play your hand out (meaning he doesn't have Blackjack) he'll bust 23 times out of 100—in the long run. Interestingly, when he has a 7 up he'll bust 26 times out of 100—not really much difference.

And when you hit 16, your own chance to bust is exactly the same whether the dealer shows a 10 or a 7—there's absolutely no difference. So far the two hands seem pretty similar for playing purposes.

But here's where there's a *big* difference. Suppose you hit your 16 and manage to dodge the bullet by catching a small card—let's say a deuce—to make 18. How does that make you feel? Good, right? The fact is, if the dealer has a 10 up, you're still probably going to lose the hand. But if you catch that same deuce against the dealer's 7 up, you're likely to be a winner! You've run exactly the same risk of busting in both situations, but you're much more likely to win the hand against the 7 than against a 10 if you don't bust! That makes hitting much more worthwhile against a dealer's 7.

When you hit 16 against a face card, in order to put you in good shape you need to catch a 4 or a 5. But against a dealer's 7, there are five different cards that will give you major help!

So trust me when I say you'll virtually always be making a very bad play whenever you lose your courage and stand with any kind of 16 against a dealer's 7.

TIP #40: If the dealer's upcard is a deuce, never soft double down. If the dealer's upcard is 5 or 6, always soft double down. If the dealers upcard is 3 or 4, play by the "rule of 9." (simply add up the total of the dealer's upcard and the "kicker" you have with your ace. If they add up to 9 or more, double down. But when the total is 8 or less, just hit the hand.) [FR]

Although most experienced blackjack players are aware of when to double down with standard totals like 10 or 11, even the most seasoned veterans tend to bungle their "soft" doubles.

Soft doubling is when you double-down with a hand like Ace/4. In the right spot, this maneuver provides a nice advantage. But in the wrong situations it's just giving money away! So let's spell out in black and white the correct hands to soft double-down with. Take a look at "Hand A" and "Hand B".

HAND "A"	HAND "B"
DEALER'S HAND	DEALER'S HAND
?/2	?/5
YOUR HAND	YOUR HAND
ACE/5	ACE/2

These hands look pretty similar for playing purposes, don't they? The problem is, *they're not!* One hand is a profitable double-down, while the other hand is a sucker's double!

What makes one hand good for soft doubling, and not the other? It's really very logical.

With Hand A, you're a 49/51 underdog. That means you'll lose the hand more often than you win it. The last thing you should do in this spot is put more money out there! With Hand B, you're a 57/43 favorite, so you definitely want to "raise the stakes."

I'm sure that many of you have seen a Basic Strategy chart and have glanced over its soft hand section. It can become pretty confusing with all of the zig-zag steps for hitting, standing, and doubling with the various soft hands. What you need is a *simpler* way to remember what to do when these situations pop up in the heat of battle.

First off, understand that the only soft hands you'll ever *consider* doubling with are when you have Ace/2 through Ace/7 against a dealer's 6 or lower. Forget about ever doubling any soft hands against a dealer that shows 7 or higher—got that? Follow the three rules above whenever you have a hand in the *potential* soft doubling category.

TIP #41: With *16* against a *10* (and only against a 10,) if your hand contains either a *4* or *5*, stand! [FR]

A player hand of 16 against a dealer's 10 is a tough hand, but it's not always an automatic "hit." Basic Strategy says to hit 16 if the dealer shows a 7 or higher. And the basic strategy is *"basically"* right here. You see, an elementary basic strategy chart is intended to keep the game as simple as possible by giving you one cut and dried play for each different hand that can come up. And that's fine, *usually.*

It's *usually* fine because most hands *are* cut and dried. But there are a few hands—just a few— that are so close that the correct play depends upon existing circumstances. Sixteen against a ten is one of those hands.

In determining the correct basic strategy play for 16 against a 10, it was found that in the long run the player will win 46 times out of 200 by standing, and 47 times out of 200 by hitting. That's a mighty close decision! Nevertheless, hitting is a hair better than standing.

But here's the catch: Basic strategy only considers *starting hands!* That means a 10/6 or 9/7, specifically. Basic strategy does not consider built-up 16's such as 8/5/3, 7/5/4, or 4/4/4/4 for that matter. That's going beyond something as "basic" as basic strategy.

Now notice the two cards that were removed from play when you hold 10/6 or 9/7. Any of them would bust a 16 if you hit and caught one. Luckily for you though, the cards remaining to be dealt have been slightly depleted of their supply of these cards, and that's the reason you should hit. But a hand like 7/5/4 is a different story in such a marginal situation! Can you see why?

It's because many of your bust cards (the 10, 6, 9, or 7) have gone back into the deck and are available for you to catch. But two of your "bail-out" cards (the 4 and 5) have been eliminated! Remember, you're talking about a situation where you were only one-half percent better off hitting than standing when you held the 10/6. This fairly subtle change swings the probability pendulum the other way!

In fact, recent studies have shown that with 16 against a 10, if your 16 contains a 4 or a 5 you usually stand a better chance of standing than hitting—even with eight decks! You don't need to have both! The mere "switcharoo" of putting a "bust" card or two back in the pack and removing a key 4 or 5 does the trick in this close situation. But if you've built something like a 6/8/2, you should still hit because you haven't drawn any cards out of play that would have done that much for your hand.

TIP #42: Be ready to react to "not-so-basic" hands when they appear, and don't abandon the correct strategy. [FR]

Let's look at some hands that can catch you *off-guard.*

Most blackjack players take pride in themselves for knowing their correct Basic Strategy. Understand, however, that there's your *"basic"* basic strategy, then you have your *"not so basic"* basic strategy. Here's what I mean.

Take a look at the four hands below. As you view each one, look at the dealer's up-card first, then your initial two-card hand. From this vantage point, quickly add one card at a time and immediately decide upon your next move—just as you would in a briskly moving live game.

PLAYER'S HAND	DEALER'S UP-CARD
A/2–A–3–A	9
4/3–3–5–A	7
5/4–6–A	10
2/3–2–4–A	2

Let's start with Hand #1: Ace/Deuce against a 9 is an easy hit. Now you catch an Ace, and the dealer beckons, "4 or 14?" So you take another hit and catch a 3. Since you should never stand on a soft 17, you immediately signal for another hit and catch an Ace. Seeing that you *finally* reached 18, you . . . . . , you . . . . . . I hope you didn't say "stand"!! If you did, shame on you! You're supposed to hit a soft 18 against a 9, even when it's the surprising five-card variety! *See how you can get caught off guard?*

Okay . . . Hand #2: You have 4/3 against the dealer's 7. Your first hit is another 3, followed by a rapid-fire 5 and followed up with an Ace. What now? You'd better say, "Hit" with *any* kind of 16 against a 7! But I've seen scores of players (who know better) soften up and stand on a l-o-n-g 16 against a 7! Don't be one of them; it's a costly mistake.

On to Hand #3: You start out with a total of 9 against the dealer's 10-point card. Your first hit is a 6, giving you 15. Then you hit again and catch an Ace to make 16, so you . . . ., you . . . . . *you didn't hit again, did you?* With a multi-card 16 against a 10, you're supposed to *stand* if your hand contains either a 4 or 5, and yours contains both!! This hand is a much, much closer decision than 16 against a 7, and it comes up about three times an hour. Don't overlook this situation when it pops up out of the blue.

Now for Hand #4: You've got the lowest unpaired start you can get—5 against the dealer's deuce. You hit and catch a deuce to make 7. The dealer doesn't even slow down because he knows you need more, and he keeps right on dealing when the next card—a 4—gives you 11. But he pauses when the next card—an Ace—brings you to 12. Now, *I* know that *you* know that you're supposed to hit that 12, *but will you??* Or will the fear of an impending face- card warp your discipline?

As you can see, basic strategy is simple; "Not-so-basic strategy" is trickier.

TIP #43: Look for a barrage of small cards on the board, then increase your bets. [FR]

Blackjack is one of the few casino games that allows you to find an "edge" by being observant.

The fact is, casino games are designed to take your money. Most of them are "bulletproof" in this regard. Even a perfect basic strategy blackjack player faces a one-half percent disadvantage to the house in a typical six-deck game. A one-half percent disadvantage means playing 200 hands and finishing one bet behind if the cards run perfectly normal. That's a close deal, but they still have ever-so-slightly the best of you.

However, blackjack does in fact have a loophole. It was probably never intended to be, but it's there. Where? Look at the following scenario:

DEALER'S HAND

5/6-4-A-5

YOU	CENTER FIELD	1st BASE
5/4-5	4/6-10	3-5-3-6 &
		3-5-10

It's the first deal off the top of a six-deck shoe. The first baseman split a pair of 3's, then drew several cards. The next player doubled-down with 10. You doubled with 9 and caught a 5. The dealer had a 5 up and proceeded to make a five card 21! As she sweeps the board the players moan in disgust. One of them storms away, hoping to avoid an impending dealer's "hot streak." The other, glad that he left, thinks that it may change the cards in the player's favor. *All nonsense!*

But here's something that isn't nonsense. High cards in blackjack help the player and low cards help the dealer. That's a fact! Now, look at the illustration again. Notice anything unusual? Out of 18 cards there were only two 10's. *With the barrage of small cards that have come out here, the players actually have a 1% advantage on the next hand!* This is something that never happens in craps, roulette, or baccarat, and an observant blackjack player can take advantage of it.

At these times you should stay put and increase your bets for the next few hands. It doesn't even have to be the beginning of a shoe. That's because anytime you see a very strong surplus of *low cards* on a full board, the remaining shoe is likely to contain at least a modest surplus of *high cards.* This is what you came for—to find an edge!

Don't go crazy however! *You can still lose six or seven consecutive hands in spite of a small advantage. This is gambling, so don't risk anything you're not willing to part with.*

Now, exactly how many extra low cards do you have to see before increasing your bet in a six-deck game? Going by generalities rather than counting each card as it's played is a vague science. But if at least 15 cards are on the board, and no less than 80% are small ones (2 through 6,) you most likely have a workable edge. Bet it up for the next few hands with the understanding that there are no guarantees.

TIP #44: Concentrate on your own hand, and don't worry about bad players. [FR]

Simple fact: Bad players cannot hurt your chances of winning!

The false belief that bad players hurt a good player's chances to win is so widespread that many die-hard "21" buffs refuse to play with novices! That's right, I said *false belief.* Furthermore, I can prove that it's false if you'll just follow along with me.

Suppose you're playing blackjack with only one other person at the table. You're at 1st base and he's at 3rd. The dealer has a deuce up. You're both dealt a 15. Acting first, you make the correct play and stand. Now it's the 3rd baseman's turn, and I bet you want him to stand too.

Why? You're afraid that if he makes a mistake and hits, he'll cause you to lose! Between fearing what the dealer might have in the hole, and what the next card out of the shoe might be—or the one after it, you wish the 3rd baseman would just "play it by the book" and stand, don't you?

Well then, let's put some of those fears to rest. First, let's take a peek at the dealer's hole card. As you can see, it's a face card, giving him 12.

DEALER'S HAND
2 / 10

3rd BASE	YOU
10 / 5	10 / 5

But let's not stop here. Now, let's bribe the dealer into flashing us a quick glimpse of the next two cards in the shoe! They're a 9 and a 10, but we couldn't tell which card was first and which was second.

NEXT TWO CARDS
9 /10 or 10 / 9

Now how do you want the 3rd baseman to play his hand? Let's see . . . If he hits, no matter which card comes first, he loses. If he stands, he's got a 50-50 shot at winning. So obviously, hitting is the wrong play for *him.* But how does that affect your chances? *Think about it.* If the 3rd baseman *stands* and 9 is first out of the shoe, the dealer makes 21. But if the 10 comes first, the dealer busts.

Now, what happens if the 3rd baseman *hits* instead of standing? Well, when he takes the 9, the dealer gets the 10 and busts. But if the 10 comes first, the dealer makes 21 with the 9! *Is the light bulb going on yet?*

Can you see that while hitting his hand is a horrible play for Mr. 3rd Base, *your* odds to win remain the same no matter what he does? That's absolutely true because your chance to win does not depend upon how the 3rd baseman plays his hand, *but upon which card is next out of the shoe!* Often, it won't matter—both cards will either make him or break him. But whenever it does matter, you never know whether you want him to get the first card or the second! Hence, being concerned over how the 3rd baseman plays is *sheer nonsense!*

BLACKJACK VARIATIONS

TIP #45: Never place a blackjack side bet! [FS]

The best rule of thumb I can give you for any new version of blackjack (or any new *game* for that matter) is . . . *change is bad!* I know that the 60s generation, of which I am an embarrassed member, preached that "change is good!" Any change, all change. "I am here to effect change," many a politician said before screwing everything up. Abraham Lincoln cautioned that the greatest threats to successful institutions of democracy will be people trying to make names for themselves by changing what works.

Of course, not all change is bad—just most!

And what holds true for society holds true for casino games—new games, or changes in old games are usually bad for the general population. You must realize that casinos put in new games and variations into old games to make more money, not less. Don't be fooled by the casino promos: "Triple your fun by playing Multiple-Action Blackjack!" A basic strategy player won't triple his fun, he'll triple his losses! I am always very leery whenever the casinos loudly announce a new variation of blackjack. Although a few have turned out to be decent games (Spanish 21 and Double Exposure, if basic strategy changes are properly applied) none can match the greatness of their progenitors.

The greatest house edges can usually be found in blackjack propositions that require a side bet (usually $1) to win a jackpot on a premium hand such as 7-7-7 of the same suit, or 6-7-8 of the same suit, etc. These are sucker bets because they appeal to narrow thinking. The sucker says to himself: "It's only a buck, and look at the giant jackpots I can win!" Keep this in mind: At a blackjack table you can play upwards of 100 hands an hour. If the side bet comes in with a house edge in the double digits, as most do, even if that edge is only 10%, you are giving the casino an extra $10 an hour for that $100 wagered! That's double what a $5 basic strategy player can expect to lose in *two hours* of play at 100 hands per hour!

Then there's the temptation to alter basic strategy and hit hands in hopes of catching the third card required for a jackpot payoff. It's difficult to compute the amount of damage resulting from these changes in basic strategy, but it's got to be harmful to your bankroll.

The only time the new variations might be helpful will be if they are given away free: no extra bets, no changes in basic playing rules, just a little gift from your friendly casino!

CRAPS

TIP #46: A: Avoid all bets in the middle of the table, and the field bet. B: Bet the pass line. C: Cheer when you win, chafe when you lose! [FS]

Craps has been a popular casino table game for zillions of years—well, not quite zillions, but long enough for even the occasional gambler to have learned the basics of the game. Craps is so simple that even an idiot can play it. Indeed, idiots play it all the time!

Once you realize that the basic game of craps is as simple as A-B-C, everything else falls into place. Here's how simple the game of craps really is.

If you take a look at the craps layout, you'll see a whole bunch of symbols in the center of the table. Ignore them. They have meaning, but they don't offer odds that allow the player a reasonable chance of winning.

Please note the double line that goes around the whole table. Note inside that line it says "Pass" and above that line it says "Don't Pass." Above that it says "Field" and you'll see a whole bunch of numbers. Ignore them, the same way you ignored the betting options in the center of the table.

Above the Field, you'll see a box that says "Come." It's one of the best bets in the casino, but I'll get to that later. This is the bottom line "how the game of craps is played" section, so you can go to a casino tonight and yell and scream with the other players, or moan and groan when the dice go the wrong way.

You now know what to avoid: The stuff in the middle of the table, and the Field. Now let's play the game.

When the last shooter has finished his roll— made his point or "sevened out," you place a bet on the Pass line—Let's say $5. The stickman (that's the guy with the stick) passes five or six dice to the shooter, who selects two dice. The stickman takes back the other dice and places them in a bowl, and the boxman (the guy who is sitting down) takes the bowl and places it near him.

Now the shooter rolls, after all bets have been placed. This is called the "come-out roll." If the shooter rolls 7 or 11, your $5 Pass line bet is paid off at even money. If the shooter rolls 2, 3, or 12, you lose your $5 Pass line bet. To continue playing, you'll have to put up another $5 Pass line bet. On the come-out roll, the Pass line bettor has the best of it because he can win eight ways on the 7 or 11, while only losing four ways on the 2, 3, or 12.

If the shooter rolls a 4, 5, 6, 8, 9, or 10— which are all those numbers in those big boxes at the top of the layout—that becomes the shooter's "point." The dealer will take a black and white "puck" and put it white-face up to indicate the point number to be made by the shooter. He now has to roll the same number again—the point number—before he rolls a 7, in order to win.

Now, the shooter rolls again. If he rolls any number but the 7 or the point number, nothing happens to your $5 Pass line bet. If he rolls the point, you win even money ($5 for your $5 bet.) If he rolls a 7, you lose your $5.

Once the shooter rolls a number, the casino's "edge" slightly improves—an edge that makes the Pass line bet lose *seven more times than it wins in 495 decisions*—not that bad, is it?

That's it. Yes, it is that simple. Everything else you will learn about craps will just refine your knowledge about the game.

TIP #47: By playing the pass line or the come bet, the casino "edge" is only 1.41%—a small disadvantage considering the simplicity of play. [FS]

Once you have the Pass line bet down cold, you might decide that you want even more action—action being defined as more money at risk with potentially more reward in the offing. To do this, and still keep the house edge low, savvy craps buffs will place a Come bet once the "point" (number) is established. Here's how it works.

The shooter is on the come-out roll. You place a Pass line bet. He rolls a 10 as his point. You now place a Come bet in the huge Come box just above the Don't Pass line. This bet functions exactly like the Pass line bet. If the shooter rolls a 2, 3, or 12, you lose your Come bet. If he rolls one of the other numbers—4, 5, 6, 8, 9, or 10—your bet is placed in box at the top of the layout corresponding to the number. Now, to win the Come bet that number must be rolled before a 7 shows. But if the 7 shows before that number, you lose. It is exactly the same situation as the Pass line. With a Pass line bet on the 10, here are the possible scenarios for a player who has put up a Come bet:

1. Shooter rolls a 7. You win the Come bet. You lose the Pass line bet. A new shooter is now on the come-out.

2. Shooter rolls an 11. You win the Come bet. No decision on the Pass line bet. You take the win, and keep the Come bet up.

3. Shooter rolls 2, 3, or 12. You lose the Come bet. No decision on the Pass line bet. You put up a new Come bet.

4. Shooter rolls a 4, 5, 6, 8, or 9. Your Come bet is moved to that number. You now have to hit that number before a 7 shows to win for the house. If a 7 is rolled you lose the Come bet, and your Pass line bet.

5. Shooter rolls a 10. You win your Pass line bet. Your Come bet goes up on the number. Even though the next roll will be a new come-out for the shooter, your Come bet will be working. If the shooter rolls a 7, you'll lose that Come bet. However, if you placed a Pass line bet, you win that wager.

Some players like to have a Pass line bet and two Come bets working at all times. This gives them more chances to win, but also more money to lose when that ugly 7 rears its miserable face.

There is a logic to being on more than one number. It's quite possible that a shooter could have a hot or even blistering roll—without once hitting his Pass line point. A shooter might get into a rhythm of hitting every number but his Pass line number. Thus, being up on two or three numbers gives you a much better chance to capitalize on a hot roll. The ecstasy of craps—those times when players are dancing and cheering—comes when the shooter keeps hitting the numbers you're on. Then craps is truly magical!

Unfortunately, the flip side to a hot roll is not so pleasant. If you are up on several numbers and that 7 hits, you lose all those bets at once! The agony of craps is that when you win, you win one bet at a time, but when you lose, you lose the whole shebang!

What's important to know is that these two bets—the Pass line bet and the Come bet—only allow the casino a small edge over you.

TIP #48: Make the lowest possible pass, don't pass, come, or don't come bets, and make the highest possible odds bets. [FS]

Here's another simple bet that's one of the best bets in the casino. Craps players can make the house edges on the Pass and Come, Don't Pass and Don't Come even lower by utilizing an option called "odds" that allows them to add money to bets that have already gone up on the numbers.

Novice players should note that casinos offer different limits on how much they can wager on the "odds" bet. There's usually a sign on the inside wall of the craps table which says, "2 Times Odds" or "5 Times Odds" or 10 Times Odds or 20 Times Odds or, holy of holies, even "100 Times Odds Offered at This Table." This sign is very important as it alerts savvy craps players to how much they can increase their bets once they are up on the Pass points, the Come numbers, the Don't Pass numbers, or the Don't Come numbers.

In a double odds (2X) game, the most common in America, a Pass line bettor is allowed to put double the amount of his Pass line wager in "odds" behind his point. Thus, if a player has $5 on the Pass line, he can put up $10 in odds once the point is established. If the casino allows 10X odds, he can put up $50. What's so good about this? THE CASINO HAS NO EDGE ON THE "ODDS" BET! They are paid off at true odds. Thus, if the point number is 4, and the player puts up $10 in odds behind his $5 Pass line bet, and the 4 hits, he receives a $20 payment for his $10 odds bet (2 to 1) and his Pass line bet is paid off at even money.

This same procedure holds true for Come bets as well. Once he is up on a number, a $5 Come player can give the dealer $10 to put on the Come bet in odds, which will be paid off at the true odds of the bet.

And what are the true odds of the various numbers? Since everything is judged against the 7, and the 7 can be made six ways out of the 36 possible combinations of two six-sided dice, we just do some simple math:

1. The number 4 can be made three ways to the 7's six ways. The 4 is therefore a 2 to 1 underdog.

2. The same holds true for the 10, which is also made three ways to the 7's six ways. So winning a $10 odds bet on 4 or 10 pays 2 to 1, or $20.

3. The 5 and 9 can each be made four ways to the 7's six ways, and are 3 to 2 underdogs. Win the $10 odds bet and you get paid three to two, or $15.

4. The 6 and 8 can each be made five ways to the 7's six ways, and therefore you are a 6 to 5 underdog. With a $10 odds bet you get $12 in return on the 6 or 8.

5. On the "Don't" side of the line, you have

to put up the long end of the bet since you are betting *with* the 7 (the favorite) and against the number (the underdog.) Reverse the bets listed above, and reverse the payoffs.

How much does the odds bet reduce the house edge? A lot! In a double odds game, the house edge drops from approximately 1.4% to .6%! In a 5X odds game, the edge drops to around .3%, while in a 20X odds game the edge plummets to around .10%—that's an expected loss of approximately a dime for every $100 bet this way!

The mathematically very best approach to craps is to bet the *least* possible amount on the Pass and Come, or the Don't Pass and Don't Come, and back them with the most possible (that you can afford) in odds. Played this way, craps now has the most sovereign sway as the lowest house-edge game in the casino!

TIP #49: If you choose to be a place better, place the 6 or 8 in multiples of $6, and avoid the other place bets. [FS]

The Pass, the Don't Pass, the Come, and the Don't Come bets are among the very best bets in the casino. And when the Odds option is exploited by a savvy player in the correct way, these bets literally become the very best bets in the casino outside of counting cards at blackjack. When you face house edges in the low tenths of a percent, you have an excellent chance of bringing home the bacon tonight—if you don't become too piggish about it.

However, not all craps players like getting up on the numbers this way. Many right-betting "action players" want to get right up on the numbers without having to go through the Pass or Come.

Their thinking is simple to follow: With Pass and Come, you have to hit the number twice before you can win anything on it. While the mathematics of the game dictates that every number is always likely to come up (now, then, or whenever) strictly in accordance with its probability, action players don't see it that way at all. They want it right now!

To accommodate such players, the casino will allow a type of wager called a "Place" bet, where you can go right up on any of the numbers without having to first go through the Pass line or Come bets. Once you Place a number, if that number hits before a 7, you win; if a 7 hits before that number, you lose.

To sweeten the pot the casino will give "house odds" on the Place bets. Recall that the Pass and Come bets are heavy favorites in their initial placements as they win eight times on the 7 and 11 and lose only four times on the 2, 3, or 12— you're a two to one favorite and you get an even-money payoff! But once on a number, that even-money payoff has dramatically deleterious effects on the Pass and Come prospects, as the 7 is now a heavy favorite to win.

No one in his or her right mind would Place a 4 or a 10 to win against a 7, if the payoff were even money. After all, a 4 is a two-to-one underdog. So the casino offers the following house odds for Placing the numbers:

9 to 5 on the 4 or 10
7 to 5 on the 5 or 9
7 to 6 on the 6 or 8

The house edge for the Placing of the 4 or 10 is a staggering 6.67%—much too big to buck. The 5 or 9 is not much better, coming in at 4%.

But, interestingly enough, the Placing of the 6 or 8 in multiples of $6 is a good bet, as the house edge is a manageable 1.52%. What does that mean? It means that for every $100 bet this way, the house is expected to win a mere $1.52. This kind of edge is not extraordinarily difficult to overcome in the short haul with a little luck, as opposed to a lot of luck you need to overcome big edges in the short run.

TIP #50: "Shop around" for the best "buy bet" opportunities. [FS]

There's another good Place bet that many novice craps players are not aware of. It's called a "Buy" bet. The traditional Buy bets are usually made by paying a 5% commission on the 4 or 10 in order to get true two-to-one odds on the bet. It works like this: I decide to Place the 4 or 10 for $20, but I pay 5% ($1) up front as a commission. (I say to the dealer, "Buy the 4 for $20!" and flip him $21.) If I win I get a payoff of $40, the true odds of the bet. The house edge has been reduced from 6.67% (outrageously rotten) to 4.76% (just rotten.)

Over the years the casinos have modified their "buys" to be even more player-friendly. You can buy the 4 or 10 for $25 and still pay $1, which reduces the house edge to 3.85%, and some casinos will allow you to bet $35 with the same $1 commission—reducing the edge to 2.78%.

Recently, some Vegas casinos decided to undercut their competition for "action" players by allowing them to Buy the 4 or 10 and only pay the commission if they won! This Buy has to be made in multiples of $25, but it reduces the house edge on buying the 4 or 10 to 1.27%—a really good bet! Now "action" players in Las Vegas might find a game that's just as good as the Pass and Come game by Placing the 6 and 8 and Buying the 4 and 10.

TIP #51: Make one "don't come" bet per shooter. [FS]

If your intention in playing craps is to win money and not friends, then there is a simple system developed by a man I call, "Darkside Sam" that can give you plenty of time at the tables with a minimum of risk and a maximum of pleasure. It can also give you a very good shot at winning some of the casino's money!

Over 90% of craps players are "right" bettors. That is, they bet with the shooter and against the 7; or they Place the numbers (4, 5, 6, 8, 9, 10) and hope they hit before the 7 shows. But there is a whole other side to craps—a side known as the Dark Side—where a player roots for the 7 and against the shooter. Players who play on the Dark Side are frowned upon by the "rightsiders," but who cares? You're there for the casino's money, not to make friends, right?

Darksiders bet Don't Pass or Don't Come, or they Lay against the numbers (also known as Placing to Lose.) It is a mirror image of the "right" side betting, and is often known as "wrong" betting. For example, on the Come Out rolls when Pass Line rightsiders are rooting for the 7 or 11 (which are immediate wins) and against the 2, 3, or 12 (which are immediate losers,) the Darksider is rooting for the 2 or 3 on which he wins, and against the 7 and 11, on which he loses (nothing happens one way or the other to the Darksider on the 12.) Once a shooter has established his point number, rightsiders are rooting for it to hit again and praying for the 7 to stay away, while darksiders are rooting for the 7 to show.

Rightsiders want "hot" shooters who roll for long periods of time without sevening out. Darksiders want a 7 as fast as the dice can form them.

Dark Side Sam has a simple system aimed at avoiding "hot" shooters and winning from the "wrong" side. Once a shooter has established his point, simply place a Don't Come bet. On the shooter's next roll, if a 7 or 11 shows, you'll lose your bet; if a 2 or 3 shows, you'll win your bet. This part of the strategy is filled with danger as there are eight ways to lose on the 7 and 11, and only three ways to win on the 2 and 3. However, if the shooter rolls any of the "point" numbers—4, 5, 6, 8, 9, 10—your Don't Come bet goes up on them. Now, you are in the driver's seat as the 7 is a decided favorite over all the other numbers: two to one against the 4 or 10; three to two against the 5 or 9; six to five against the 6 or 8.

That's Dark Side Sam's simple system. You bet one Don't Come bet against every shooter. If you win, you wait for the next shooter. If you lose, you wait for the next shooter. Often a win will herald a new shooter since most wins will be when a shooter sevens-out.

You don't need a huge bankroll to play this way. Have enough to make 15 Don't Come bets and you should have enough to last a few hours at the table and have a decent chance to take home some money. The casino only has a 1.4% edge on you betting this way. That is very, very low.

A word of caution: Do not, I repeat, do not go up on the Don't Pass, as the shooter can clobber you with a series of 7s and 11s on the Come-Out roll if you persist on betting against him.

"LIVE" POKER

TIP #52: In 5 card draw, usually fold anything less than a pair of kings.

TIP #53: In 7 card stud, usually fold anything less than a pair of nines, a small pair with a queen minimum kicker, a three card flush, or a three card straight.

TIP #54: In texas hold'em, fold most hands that do not contain a pair, two high cards, or a suited ace.

TIP #55: In omaha hi-lo, fold most hands that do not contain an ace/deuce, a pair of aces, or four cards all 6 or lower. [FR]

Make no mistake about it—poker is a game of skill. At every table there is a best player and a worst player. In fact, there's an old poker adage that says, "*After playing your first few hands, take a look around the table and try to spot the 'sucker.' If you don't see any—it's you!*"

But what separates a good poker player from a bad one? The number one mistake that bad poker players make is playing too many hands. Why is this such a deadly error? Two very important reasons:

1. In most casino poker games, eight or nine hands are usually dealt, but only one can win the pot.

2. The best hand going in is usually the best hand coming out.

So what does this mean? Throw away all but your best starting hands—right now! Whether to play the very first bet is usually the most important decision of the entire hand. If you don't have the best hand out of the gate—or a clear shot at making the best hand—it'll only cost you money if you continue to play.

A general rule of thumb is that you should be throwing away the bottom 75% of all of your starting hands without calling a bet. And with many of the remaining 25%, you'll fold before the hand is over.

Bear in mind that unlike most gambling games, proper strategy in poker is in a continuous state of flux. Some hands that are worth a raise in one spot should be folded in another. So with this thought in mind, the preceeding are a few *rough* examples of minimum starting hand requirements for several of the more common games. Patterning your play along these lines will get you to dump your "sucker" hands at the onset.

TIP #56: When all the cards have been dealt, and you have the high hand on the board: if the full strength of your hand is showing, *check!* [FR]

Let's talk about one of the most common faults among inexperienced poker players: Knowing when *not* to bet. One of their most common faults is their inability to recognize when it's *wrong* to bet with a good hand. When would that be? Take a look at the following scenario:

The game is Seven Card Stud. All seven

cards have been dealt, and you have one remaining opponent. Your three hole cards consist of two queens and a jack, and your four exposed cards consist of a pair of 10s and a pair of Aces. Your opponent's hand shows a pair of Queens, plus a 2 and a 7, with no matching suits. You started out with a 10/Jack/Queen, and proceeded to make open Aces and 10s on the board. Since you're high, it's up to you to bet or check. What's the correct play? (Suggestion: Before you answer this question, take a deck of cards and construct these two hands in front of you.)

Let's analyze it. If your opponent has just a pair of Queens, or even Queens up, you have him beaten. He can't possibly have three Queens since you hold the other two Queens in your hand. It's also impossible for him to have a straight or a flush. The only way you can lose is to something like a full house—7s over Queens—or four 2s! You're the odds-on favorite to have the best hand, yet *betting in this spot is positively wrong!* Why? Because the entire virtual strength of your hand is exposed, thus *you'd be making a bet that you can lose but cannot win!*

You see, noboby's getting any more cards. The winning hand, whichever it is, has already been dealt. At this point, a bet on your part can no longer help you win the pot. Think about it. If you bet, your opponent will certainly not fold if he has a full house. Also, he won't call with Queens up, since he's already looking at your Aces up.

If you bet in this spot, usually your opponent will just fold, and you'll rake in a pot that would have been yours even if you had checked. *But the pot will not contain his last call!*

However, for that one odd time when he has a full house or four 2s, you'll lose a pot that you were going to lose anyway, *plus the last bet that you never could have won!*

Checking is the correct play in this case because *you will only be called if you are beaten.* You have nothing to gain by betting, but you do have something to lose—*the last bet on the end.*

TIP #57: If your pot odds are higher than your odds against winning a pot, play out the hand. If they're lower, fold! [FR]

In any poker game, you must be aware of the "pot odds." That tells you what's worth the risk and what's not. That's what it all comes down to. Here's a good example:

Suppose you're playing live Draw Poker, Jacks or better to open. The stakes are $5 before the draw and $10 after. Seven players ante $1 each, the cards are dealt, and everyone passes around to you. Squeezing out your hand you find a: *6-7-8-9-Q,* which you must also pass since you don't have Jacks or better. The player after you is dead last, and opens for $5. One by one, everybody else folds until it's just the opener and you. Should you call, raise, or fold?

The absolutely correct play is to fold! Why? Because if you call and draw one card you'll only make the straight one time out of six. And when you do, you'll have to win back all the money you lost the other five times, or you're playing a losing game of poker!

It's not that hard to figure out why you should fold. Let's assume that if you make your straight, you'll win the $7 that was in the ante, plus your opponent's $5 opening bet, plus a $10 call from him after the draw. That's a potential gain of

$22—the one time out of six that you make the straight. But you'll lose $5 each of the other five times, resulting in $25 in losses and you being a net overall loser! It's not that you should never draw to an open-end straight in poker. It's just that in this situation, you're not getting good enough *odds from the pot to go for it!*

Sometimes it's wrong to draw to an open-end straight, and sometimes it's right to try for an inside straight—it mostly depends upon your *"pot odds."* They must be higher than your odds of winning the pot, or it's just not worth the gamble.

Here's an opposite example: Suppose you're playing a Seven Card Stud hand. There were initially lots of callers, but by the time the sixth card has been dealt you're in there all alone with one opponent who is showing *5,4,8,Ace* on board. As he tosses a $10 bet into the pot, he accidentally tips his hole cards, revealing a *6,7* for an eight-high straight. You hold *Q,Q,9,K,3,10.* Due to the earlier betting, there's $125 in the pot. Now it's definitely correct to pay $10 to try for the inside straight— the Jack—on the last card. If you hit it, you'll get 13 or 14 to 1 on an 11 to 1 shot! Remember: At the end of your poker life, your net result will merely be made up of a blend of all the *pot odds* you were receiving along the way.

TIP #58: Fold, bet, or raise a lot; but call only sparingly. [FR]

Every time there's a bet made to you in a hand of poker you have three options: call, raise, or fold. How often should each of them be done? Let's look at a common example.

Suppose you're playing $5 and $10 Seven

Card Stud. All eight players have anted 50 cents each. The low card, a deuce, is forced in for $2. Looking down, you have a split pair of 8s with a 10 kicker. One by one, the other players fold and the bet finally gets around to you. What should you do?

YOU SHOULD RAISE!

Why? Because you probably have the best hand and there's $6 in the pot for somebody to take. If the deuce wants to play with you, let him pay for it. If he doesn't, you make a quick six bucks; simple!

Now let's play that same hand over again with a little different twist. This time as the $2 bet is coming around towards you and you're getting ready to raise, a player with a King showing beats you to it and raises first. Then the next player with a Jack up calls. Now what's your best move?

YOU SHOULD FOLD!

Why? Because the King is already telling you he has some kind of playable hand and it might well be a pair of Kings! That combined with the call by the Jack leaves you too defenseless with your wimpy 8s and an undercard kicker.

Very often in poker, your hand may start out to look pretty good and be worth raising with. But then, somebody else with stronger looking potential does the raising first, and suddenly your hand isn't even worth a call! It happens all the time!

You see, calling in poker is usually a lame play. It might be fine in sociable "kitchen table" games, but is serious casino poker a chronic caller is a chronic loser! Why? Because raising gives you two ways to win: when they don't call you, and when you make the winning hand.

Whenever you have a hand that you feel is worth a call, you should consider raising! If you don't think you can profitably raise, there's a fair chance you shouldn't even be calling. Most of the time, in most poker games, you should be folding or raising.

Yes, there *are* some appropriate calling situations, such as when you're on the come with a flush or a straight draw. Another calling spot would be at the end of a hand where an opponent bets into you, and you have only a *decent* hand that may or may not be the winner.

TIP #59: Never underestimate the "rake." By-pass the $1–$5 games in favor of the $5 & $10 stakes, then play *very* tight. [FR]

Another thing you must never do is underestimate the "rake." Every casino game has a built-in house edge somewhere. In roulette, it's the zero and double-zero. In blackjack it's the fact that the dealer wins if you bust first, even if she busts later. But where's the house edge in casino poker? Isn't poker a "zero sum" game?

Played at your kitchen table, yes—it's a zero sum game. That means all the money that the players *bring* to the game leaves the game *with* the players, only redistributed. But since the casino doesn't "play" in casino poker, it has to make money by charging the players to play against each other. That's called the "rake." And at the lower stakes games, the rake is your deadliest adversary, rather than the other players!

Casinos have two or three different methods of raking their poker games, but the most common is to take a "cut" out of each pot. Here's a typical example: The lowest stakes game in most casinos today is a $1 - $5 Seven Card Stud game. The pots generally reach about $40, and the house will typically rake $4 out of each pot.

If that 10% rake doesn't sound like much, then answer this riddle: *If eight players sat down with $50 each, and were dealt 25 hands per hour while $4 was raked out of each pot, after four hours how many winners could there be?* The answer is NONE!! The house would have raked the whole $400 off the table!!

How can you fight that? There are only two ways. First, in these low-stakes games you need to play very tight, winning only a modest number of pots—but a high percentage of the ones you're in. Starting with nothing but quality hands will keep your "batting average" high, but your "tax" low.

The second way to minimize the effects of the rake is to play for somewhat higher stakes. $1 - $5 poker is very cheap gambling anyway. In total dollar volume it's about the equivalent of playing blackjack for $2 per hand.

But in a $5 to $10 poker game, the rake is not allowed to exceed $5. Those pots generally reach $90 or $100—and the rake "percentage" is practically cut in half!

Now let's reconstruct the riddle from above—this time adjusting everything proportionally to a $5 & $10 game. Eight players buy in for $125 each and are dealt 25 hands per hour, while $5 gets raked from each pot. After the same four hours, there's still $500 on the table. Now there's room for a couple of winners!

At higher stakes yet, the rake counts even

less, but the skill of your opposition goes way up! Thus, you may find yourself "in over your head."

TIP #60: With two small pair, raise to get it heads up, open from a late seat, or throw the hand away. [FR]

Let's talk about draw poker. Five Card Draw is about the most basic poker game around. There just aren't that many different facets to its strategy.

A critical phase of your Draw Poker repertoire arises when you have two small pair. In fact, how you play two small pair may determine whether you'll be a long term winner or loser at the game.

As hard as it is to be dealt two pair in five cards (only 5% of the time,) two *small* pair is unlikely to win the pot if there are a lot of callers. In Jacks or Better to open, for example, what should you do if you are dealt 8's and 6's? Actually, you should almost always either *fold* or *raise*, depending upon your position from the dealer. *Just calling with them is usually suicide.*

Let's get specific. Suppose you're first to act with those 8's and 6's. You have openers, but can't stand much action. Your correct play is to *check* (pass) and not open. Now, watch closely as the action moves around the table. If somebody opens (signifying Jacks or better) and there are any callers, when it comes back to you, *fold!* Two small pair probably won't stand up in a three or four way pot, and you'll make a full house only one time in twelve!

Instead, suppose the hand gets opened from a late seat, and nobody else is in when it gets back to you. Now you must *raise!* The opener

most likely has one high pair, and you need to discourage other potential callers from coming in
and drawing against you. If you don't protect your
hand in this way, you're going to be shown an
awful lot of "Jacks up" and "Queens up" hands
after the draw.

Now what if you're in a late seat yourself
with those same small 2 pair? Simple! If nobody's
opened yet, go ahead and open it. If it has been
opened and nobody's called yet, raise it! But if it's
been both opened and called, fold! Notice that
what you're striving to do is get it heads up against
one player. Sometimes due to circumstances beyond your control, you'll find yourself in there with
two opponents. But you must do what you can to
keep the field thin.

Now what happens if you open or raise with
two small pair and get raised yourself? Unless you
know your opponent to be a wild man, give it up!
You'll almost always be up against a better hand
than your own, and remember—it's hard to improve two pair.

What do you do if you're dealt three of a
kind on your first five cards in Draw Poker? This is
a pretty strong hand, and it'll win without improvement the vast majority of times. But since Draw
Poker is only a two bet game, you should generally
play it fast before the draw in order to get some
money in the pot. That means raising immediately,
since oftentimes you won't be able to gain a call
after the draw when your opponents fail to improve
their one-pair hands.

If you're in an early seat however, it's usually
better not to open yourself. Since few pots get
"passed out," you should normally check (pass)
from an early position, then check-raise after somebody else opens. It's rare that your opponent will

open, then fold without at least calling your raise to draw to his hand (although that would often be the correct move). By the way, I want to stress that, unlike two pair, it's right to come in raising even if there's an opener and a couple of callers. Trips are that much stronger of a hand!

TIP #61: Draw 1 card to trips! [FR]

A better question however, is how do you draw to your trips? In most cases, *you should draw just one card!* That's right. Your chances of improvement aren't very different whether you draw one card or two (when you draw two cards, you'll improve 1 time in 10—drawing one, you'll improve 1 time in 12,) and you probably don't need to improve anyway!

But here's where drawing one card helps. Suppose somebody opens in Jacks or Better, and you raise with:

$$5\text{-}5\text{-}5\text{-}4\text{-}9$$

The opener calls your raise and draws three cards. Now you draw one card, representing that you have only two pair. The opener simply must have one big pair and will *at least* call if he makes a second pair. Better yet, if he opened with something like a pair of Aces and makes Aces up, he'll probably bet out himself figuring he has your two pair beaten, and you can now raise! Had you drawn two cards after you raised on the open, your opponent would have feared trips and probably just checked, then called with his two big pair. *Drawing one card to trips will often gain you an extra bet!*

About the only time you should draw two

cards to trips is when you fear that your hand needs help. For example, suppose somebody opens and you raise with those three 5's, then the opener re-raises you! Now you probably want to draw two cards for a couple of reasons. The first would be to maximize your chances of improvement. The second is that tipping your opponent that you have trips yourself may discourage him from betting after the draw (perhaps wondering whose trips are higher.) You'd generally prefer that he not come out betting in this case.

TIP #62: In Texas Hold'em, fold any *unpaired*, *unsuited*, *non-runner* hand lower than king/10. [FR]

Let's take a look at Texas Hold'em, which is one of the most widely played poker games in public card rooms across the country. It's fast and relatively simple to understand, but playing this game *well* is another matter. With only two cards in your hand and the other five board cards shared by all, many Hold'em beginners pay to see the "flop" (three cards turned face-up on the board) too routinely. This is far from correct, since some two-card starting hands will win seven or eight times as often as others. You *must* be very finicky about which two cards you need before you'll call to see the flop. So where do we start?

First, Texas Hold'em is basically a *high* card game. An Ace/King in the hole is a better hand than a pair of 5's. Why? If you call the flop with a pair of 5's and don't hit a third 5 (an 8 to 1 shot), you almost can't win. But if you have Ace/King in the "pocket," one-third of the time there will be an Ace or a King in the flop. Then you'll have the top pair! On average, one high pair takes the pot in this game.

So when you're looking for hands worthy of calling a flop bet, big pairs in the hole (Aces through Jacks) are most desirable, followed by two very high cards (Ace/King, Ace/Queen, or King/Queen.) Everything else depreciates from there.

Two other characteristics that will make your starting hand a bit more playable or if it's suited, or contains two "runners" (two cards in numerical succession.) With a Queen/10 of clubs, for example, if the flop contains two clubs you have a four-card flush and will make your flush one-third of the time, besides having two high cards to pair. Smaller suited hands, however—such as the 9/7 of diamonds—are sucker's bait!

If you hold two high "runners" like 10/Jack, a flop of 8/9/*anything*, 9/Queen/*anything*, or Queen/King/*anything* will give you an open-end straight draw which will also fill in one-third of the time (besides your pairing possibilities.)

If you play with less than two picture cards, it's going to be very hard to feel comfortable about your hand once the flop comes down.

TIP #63: Bet/raise if you flop two pair, bet/call with a flush or straight draw, and check/fold most other hands. [FR]

The preceeding are a few tips for playing after the "flop."

Once you pick a legitimate hand to get in there with, you need to decide whether to continue after the three card flop comes down. This is where poker becomes a real game of skill. Let's run through most of the potential scenarios:

1. If you've started with a big pair, like *two Queens* in the pocket, you should have come in raising. This accomplishes two things: First, it gets more money in the pot when you most likely have the best hand. Second, it discourages stragglers from calling with something like *Jack/8*. Now, if the flop is something typical like:

JACK/8/4

you have an overpair to the board! If it's checked to you, bet. If there's a bet, raise! It's that straightforward! Keep betting until a card comes that's an overcard to your Queens, or pairs the board (giving somebody potential trips.)

2. If you came in with a small pair such as *two 6's* and the flop is that same *Jack/8/4,* you're going to have to check and then fold if anybody bets. It's just too unlikely that you have the best hand, and improving on the next card is a 22 to 1 shot! With a small pair, you're basically looking to flop trips, or dump it.

3. What if you have two high cards like *King/Queen,* and the *Jack/8/4* flops? It sort of depends . . . You see, you're not entirely out of it. On the next card, any *10, Queen,* or *King* will give you either the top pair or an open-end straight draw. All that's about a 4 to 1 shot. If there's a bet but no raise, call.

4. Now suppose you have a suited hand like the *Ace/8 of spades* when the flop comes *Jack/8/4* and no spades. Check, and if there's a bet, fold the hand, because pairing your *Ace* on the next card is a 15 to 1 shot! However, if that *Jack/8/4* contains one spade, it's worth calling one bet (but not a

raise) to see if fourth street is *either* an *Ace* or a *spade.* Of course, if the flop already contains two spades, you should go all the way.

5. About the lowest unsuited runners you should see the flop with would be *9/10.* If you have that, and the *Jack/8/4* flops, you've got a playing hand (a straight draw.) If the flop should come *7/8/4,* or *Jack/Queen/4,* you like that too! But you'd most like to see something like *10/8/4,* giving you two top pair.

TIP #64: With Omaha Hi-Lo Split, play very *low* cards, very *high* cards, or a pair of *kings* or *aces*—but no *middle* cards! [FR]

Let's look at a wild and crazy game: Omaha Hi-Lo Split. Of all the games played in public poker rooms, Omaha Hi-Lo Split provides the most action. It's dealt just like Hold'em, except that you get four cards in your hand—but you can only use two!

After all five board cards are dealt, you combine any two from your hand with any three from the board to make your best *high* hand. Then you combine any two from your hand with any three from the board to make your best *low* hand.

Ace/2/3/4/5 is the perfect low hand, as well as a *5 high straight* high hand. If one player has the best high and the best low, he gets the whole pot! However, the low hand must be an *8 or lower,* or the high hand gets it all! Thus, the game is also known as *"Omaha 8 or Better."*

Because of its "2 from the hand; 3 from the board" concept, a good starting Omaha Hand is quite different from that in most poker games. *Three of a Kind* in your hand is absolutely worthless since you can only use two cards! A *four-flush* isn't much good either, for the same reason.

In this game, you want to begin with cards that can easily combine with the future board to make both a good high and a good low hand. The Ace is a key card since it goes both ways.

Desirable components are an *Ace-deuce* (with the Ace suited,) a pair of *Aces* or *Kings,* very *high* cards, or very *low* cards. Avoid *middle* cards like the plague! As an example, suppose you were dealt a versatile starting hand like:

ACE/2/10/JACK

including the *Ace/10 of hearts.* Now, you can only use two cards from your hand to go high or low. *But you can interchange them any way you see fit to go both ways!* So let's say the flop comes down:

3/8/9 with two hearts

Although you have no complete hand just yet, you did flop enormous potential! This is the nature of Omaha-8. You usually don't have that much right on the flop, but it's your "live combinations" that make your hand good or bad.

In this case, the *3* and the *8* gives you a four-card *perfect low draw* (using your *Ace-deuce.)* The two hearts give you a *Ace high flush draw* (using your *Ace/10 of hearts.)* And the *8/9* gives you the best possible straight (using your *10/Jack.)* Any *4, 5, 6, 7, Queen,* or *heart* on either of the last two board cards will make one or more of your hands. That's two shots at 24 cards! This is a raising hand!

But without the versatility of your starting cards, it would be nearly impossible to have so much going for you on the flop.

ROULETTE

TIP #65: Play at single-zero wheels where available. [JG]

A casino table games director once told me that he was thinking of putting a single-zero roulette wheel in his high-limit pit. "I probably won't do it, though," he told me. "It doesn't seem to make any difference to the guests. Some even complain that there's no double-zero. It's their lucky number."

In reality, zero and double-zero are the players' unlucky numbers. The house edge is derived from their presence. Most payoffs at roulette are set so they would be even bets if there were 36 numbers on the wheel. But zero and double-zero make it 38 numbers. That leaves a house edge of 5.26% on almost every bet on the layout.

When there is only one zero and no double-zero, there are only 37 numbers on the wheel, close enough to the 36 on which payoffs are based that the house edge is slashed nearly in half. On a single-zero wheel, instead of giving the house $5.26 per every $100 bet, players spot the house only $2.70 per $100.

That's a difference worth the trouble of a little search.

TIP #66: Play low-limit roulette for fun; the house edge is too high for serious play. [JG]

House edges matter. When you read that the house edge on the Banker bet in baccarat is 1.17% and the house edge at double-zero roulette is

5.26%, understand that given an equal number of wagers, roulette will gobble up your bankroll nearly five times as fast as baccarat. Play 100 hands of baccarat at $10 per hand, and on the average you'll leave $11.17 behind. Make it 100 spins on the wheel instead, and you'll drop $52.60!

There might be wins at either game, of course, and there might be greater losses. But roulette's constant 5.26% drain depletes your bankroll far too quickly to be risking the big bucks. Save your big bets for games that give you more of a fighting chance.

TIP #67: Don't make the five-number bet. [JG]

Almost all roulette bets are paid at odds that would yield an even game if there were only 36 numbers on the wheel. Let's imagine a perfect sequence in which each number shows. Make single-number bets on 17 on every spin, and you win once. You're paid 35 to 1, so you have 36 units—your 35 in winnings plus the original wager that is returned to you. Make corner bets on 1, 2, 4, and 5, and you win four times at 8 to 1 payoffs. You get 32 units, plus the 4 winning wagers are returned, so you receive a total of 36 units. Bet on Red, and you win 18 times at even money. You get 18 units in winnings plus your 18 units in wagers on the winners—you're left with 36 units.

There's one exception to the above scenarios. The five-number bet on 0, 00, 1, 2, and 3 are paid at 6 to 1. In our perfect sequence of spins, it would win five times, giving you 30 units in winnings plus the one-unit bets returned on each of the five winning wagers. Your total at the end of the sequence is 35 units, *or one less than any other bet on the table!*

On a double-zero wheel, every wager but one carries a house edge of 5.26%. The one exception is the five-number bet, with a house edge of 7.89%. That'll put a big dent in your bankroll in a hurry!

Part III:
TIPS FOR MACHINE GAMES

As we enter the twenty-first century, it's interesting to note that mechanical gambling devices became popular at the start of the previous century. One hundred years of technological development and improvement has resulted in slot and video poker machines that now occupy as much as 70% of the floor space in many casinos. Players like the machines, and casinos profit from their efforts to beat them.

Why so popular? Because many gamblers don't choose to learn the intricacies of table games, and don't enjoy the confrontational aspects of competing against the dealer or other players. It's Man (or Woman) against a machine—and we're superior . . . Right?

In truth, many machine games offer better chances of winning than many of the table games. In this chapter, the experts tell you how to find the best machines, and how to maximize your chances of beating them!

SLOT MACHINES

TIP #68: Read the "glass" and/or the "help" menu before you play slot machines. [JG]

Slot machines are the easiest games to play anywhere in the casino. Just drop a coin or three in the slot, push the button or pull the handle, and you're ready to win, right?

But if you leave it at that, you'll miss out on some important information. Is there a "banked bonus" that builds as you play, leaving a profit-making opportunity? Is there a penalty on the pay table for playing less than maximum coins? On modern multiline video slots, just how are the pay-lines set up? Are there second-screen bonuses and "scatter" pays? Just what is a scatter pay, anyway?

Read the glass on the machine before you play, and it should answer your questions. On video slots, the information may be on a "help" screen in-stead, just like on your friendly home computer. Touch the "Help" button on the screen for explana-tions.

Understanding the ins and outs of a particu-lar machine before you play can alert you to the op-portunities for profit, and point out some potential pitfalls.

TIP #69: Don't play progressive or "buy-a-pay" machines with less than maximum coins. [JG]

How do you think it would feel to hit the top jackpot combination on a machine advertising a prize of $10,000, $100,000, even $1 million, and walk away with only a few thousand quarters?

84

Worse, how'd you like to hit three jackpot symbols and walk away with a big fat zero?

It happens, and I've been witness to both. A slot host once pointed out to me a fellow who had to settle for a pile of quarters instead of a check for $250,000 because he had bet only one coin in a progressive slot machine. If he had bet the maximum three quarters, he'd have struck it rich instead of winning enough for a nice dinner.

That's the major pitfall with progressive slot machines, which add a percentage of coins wagered to the jackpot that eventually will go to a big winner. If you don't bet the max, you're not eligible for the big hit.

Other machines, call "buy-a-pays" in the casino industry, have the player "buy" a set of symbols or a payline with each coin. I once saw a woman wondering where all the bells, whistles, and money were when she hit three jackpot symbols. She'd bet one coin which activated the cherries, but bet neither a second coin to activate the bars or a third coin to activate 7's and jackpot symbols. If she hit any winner except cherries, she was out of luck—she hadn't bought her paylines. Three jackpot symbols were just another losing spin. How do you avoid her fate? Move to a different machine if you're going to play less than maximum coins.

TIP #70: Never force play because you think a machine is "due to hit." [JG]

"I've been playing all day and I haven't hit a thing!" is a common complaint I hear from slot players. But when I ask why they've stayed all day at such a cold machine, too often the response is, "I figure it's due."

Slot machines are never "due" to hit. Results are determined by a random number generator—a program on a computer chip inside the machine. The random number generator continually runs through numbers that correspond to potential reel combinations, and it's running even when the machine is not in use.

It's as random as humans can design a computer program to be. The result of one push of the button or pull of the handle has no effect on the outcome of the next. Every play is a fresh start.

The net effect is that a machine is never "due" to hit. The odds are the same on every pull, and there's no use chasing past losses. There's a good chance you'll just compound your misery.

TIP #71: Seek out machines with partially completed bonuses. [JG]

Think of games that give the player a chance to gain an edge on the house . . . Blackjack, some video poker games, horse and sports betting by shrewd handicappers, slot machines . . .

Wait a minute! Slot machines?

Yes! Some modern machines that include banked bonuses give the astute player an edge— some of the time. A banked bonus is one that builds until it is won, or involves a game-within-a-game that pays a bonus when completed.

An example of a bonus that builds is the Williams reel-spinning slot *Piggy Bankin'*. When three blank spaces land on the pay line, a coin is added to a piggy bank on a Dotmation screen. When "Break the Bank" lands on a payline, the player collects the bonus in the bank. If the bank gets large enough—about 18 coins on a dollar machine, more on a quarter machine—a player who plays one coin at a time has an edge.

An example of a game-within-a-game is *Fort Knox* on the high-tech Odyssey video machines. As the player spins the video reels, he also is trying to match numbers in a 10-digit code to open the vault at Fort Knox. Find a machine with five digits matching the code, and you have an edge on the game.

Such games as these have given rise to a new breed of slot pros, who hop from casino to casino, seeking out games that have uncollected bonus potential—games that give them an edge. They play until they hit the bonus, then move on.

Most recreational slot players won't play like the pros, but they should take the hint—When choosing among machines that have banked bonuses, give yourself a head start.

TIP #72: Seek out tournaments that offer 100% equity. [JG]

Slot tournaments have become one of the most popular casino promotions. They're easy to play—Pay your entry fee, tap the button continuously to keep the reels spinning, and see how many points you can accumulate. Cash prizes are awarded to the leaders.

A few tournaments require that you put money in the machines during tournament play. Avoid these events. The best tournaments are cashless. They include play in the entry fee; you don't take cash out of the machines, but you don't put in, either. The best tournaments have free entry, but you'll have to be a big enough player in the sponsoring casino to get invited to a "freebie."

For most of us, the best we can hope for are

tournaments with 100% equity, which means that all entry fees are returned to players as cash prizes. The casino usually throws in perks, such as complimentary rooms, meals, and tournament T-shirts.

There is no house edge in a cashless, 100% equity tournament. It's a pure promotion, designed to show off the casino or reward you for your past patronage. That makes it an event well worth your while.

TIP #73: The higher the denomination of the machine, the higher the payback percentage. [JG]

Each and every slot machine is expected to pay its own keep. It must earn enough to pay for its purchase price and upkeep, and make a profit for the casino. Not only that, it cost just as much to purchase and maintain a nickel machine as it does to purchase and maintain a dollar machine.

What's a casino to do? Easy answer. Squeeze a few extra pennies out of low-denomination machines by returning a lower percentage of wagers to players. On the average, players on the Las Vegas Strip get back nearly 96% of everything they put into dollar machines, between 93% and 94% on quarter machines, and only about 90% on nickel machines.

This pattern holds up in the rest of the country, although in most jurisdictions the payback percentages are slightly lower than they are in Nevada.

One warning: Even if you're getting a higher payback percentage, your average loss per pull is higher on a higher denomination machine. Lose 5% of a dollar on a 95% payback machine and you lose more money than 10% of a nickel on a 90% payback machine. But if you have the bankroll to play the percentages, the higher denomination machines offer a higher percentage return.

TIP #74: Machines with big jackpots usually have low hit frequencies. [JG]

Slot directors have a continuing dilemma: Does it attract more business to give a really big jackpot to one player, or to give frequent smaller paybacks to lots of players? Players are attracted by big jackpots—tell me you've never been tempted as the multimillion-dollar progressive award builds at *Megabucks*—but frequent small hits seem to do better at keeping us in our seats. All we need is a little positive reinforcement every now and again.

Not only that, the money to fund the jackpot, the smaller hits, and the profit for the house has to come from somewhere . . . your pocket, for instance! It's very difficult to make the mathematics work so that a machine can offer a big jackpot, pay off frequent little hits, and still earn its keep. So, machines with smaller jackpots will usually pay off more in between jackpots than machines with larger jackpots.

VIDEO POKER

TIP #75: Learn Jacks or Better strategy first. [JG]

Every video poker player striving to improve his game has to start somewhere. The place to start is with Jacks or Better.

It may seem like you're navigating a video poker jungle in choosing among Bonus Poker, Bonus Poker Deluxe, Double Bonus Poker, Double Double Bonus Poker, and other permutations. But most games are based on Jacks or Better. You'll be ahead of the game if you learn Jacks or Better first, then tackle strategy adjustments for your other games of choice.

For example, take Double Bonus Poker: In its full-pay 10-7 version, meaning it pays 10-for-1 on full houses and 7-for-1 on flushes, it returns 100.2% with expert play. Expert play includes some odd little things, such as breaking up a full house that includes three Aces to chase a 160-for-1 jackpot on four Aces, or holding three parts of a flush with no high straight or high pair possibilities.

But let's say you play expert level 9-6 Jacks or Better, paying 9-for-1 on full houses and 6-for-1 on flushes. Expert strategy on that game yields 99.5% payback in the long run. If you simply apply Jacks or Better strategy to 10-7 Double Bonus, what do you think you get? How about 99.8%? Expert strategy at the most basic video poker game works even better at Double Bonus than on the game for which it was devised. Adjusting for all of the little quirks that stem from the Double Bonus pay table net you another 0.4%, making Double Bonus a 100.2% game. But it all starts with Jacks or Better, just as it does on most video poker games.

TIP #76: Games with big bonus payoffs have more volatile short-term results. Play Jacks or Better if you can't handle the potential big swings in fortune. [JG]

Would you rather play a game that will give you a good run for your money, letting you play for a long time on a small investment, or would you rather risk faster losses while hoping for bigger rewards?

You can have it either way with video poker. Jacks or Better is an even-keel game, while Double Bonus Poker is more of a roller coaster ride, and Double Double Bonus is a bungee jump!

How can you tell the difference? Look at the pay tables. The big payoff on all games is for a royal flush, but the bonus games put more of their return into large secondary jackpots, while even-keel games return more at the bottom of the pay table.

Jacks or Better pays 2-for-1 on two pair, while Double Bonus and Double Double Bonus pay only 1-for-1. That drop accounts for about 12% of the overall payback. The big bonus games then give back that 12% in bonuses on less common hands. Double Bonus enhances straights, flushes, full houses, and four of a kind, while Double Double enhances on the "quads" (four of a kind.)

Bet five coins per hand and draw four Aces with a deuce, and it's going to be worth 125 coins on Jacks or Better, 800 coins on Double Bonus, and 2,000 coins on Double Double Bonus. That can lead to some spectacular wins on the bonus games.

On the other hand, draw the far more common two pair on Jacks or Better, and you get 10 coins back, while you get only 5 on Double Bonus or Double Double Bonus. That means that on Jacks or Better you're getting more returns on small hands to keep you going, while on Double Bonus or Double Double Bonus you're in trouble if you don't hit the big one.

Which way is better? That's up to you. Do you prefer a good long run, or a wild ride?

TIP #77: Compare pay tables before you play comparable video poker machines. [JG]

We can tell by looking at video poker machines which are high-paying games and which are coin gobblers. They differ from slot machines, where identically-looking machines can have wildly different payback percentages. In video poker, payback percentages are changed by varying the pay tables that are either painted on the machine glass or displayed on the video screen.

Most video poker games vary the percentages by changing the payoffs on full houses and flushes. A 9-6 Jacks or Better game—the numbers refer to the payoffs on full houses or flushes per coin wagered—will pay more than an 8-5 version, which will pay more than one that cuts payoffs still further to 7-5. Same with Double Bonus Poker. If all other places on the table are equal, a 10-7 game will pay more than a 9-7 game, which will pay more than a 9-6 game.

You'll often see high and low-paying versions of the same game in the same casino. Many players don't distinguish between the two versions of the same game. One of my favorite haunts has 9-6 Jacks or Better on single-hand dollar machines, but also has a horrendous 6-5 version on quarter Triple Play Poker machines, on which the player plays three hands at once. Guess which machine I play?

The best machines even yield an edge to the player who applies expert strategy. The most common game with an edge to expert players is most likely to be 10-7 Double Bonus Poker, with its 100.2% return with its best pay table. Nevada players should seek out the 100.8% full-pay version of Deuces Wild.

It's the player's responsibility to scope out the pay tables, and walk away from the games that offer you less for your money.

TIP #78: Given equal pay tables, play maximum coins at lower denominations instead of fewer coins on higher denominations. [JG]

You've scoped out a casino, and found that it offers 9-6 Jacks or Better on both quarter and dollar machines. You're not really comfortable playing $5 a hand, so you'll not be making maximum bets on the dollar machines. Is it OK to play one coin at a time on the dollar machine instead of heading to the quarter machines? After all, it's the same game, right?

Actually it's not the same game because video poker pay tables build in an extra award for playing maximum coins. On most machines, with five coins wagered, a royal flush pays 4,000 coins— a cool $1,000 on quarter games. With fewer than five coins bet, a royal returns only 250-for-1. So if you hit a royal with only one coin bet on a dollar machine, you get $250 back, but for a quarter more, with $1.25 wagered on a quarter machine, your royal flush pays $1,000.

On this, and nearly all other video poker games, long-term payback percentage on the fifth-coin wager exceeds 100%. The casino makes its money on your first four coins: you get some of it back on the fifth coin.

93

TIP #79: Take time to clear your head before you switch games. [JG]

Switching from game to game isn't always the easiest thing to do. If you've been playing Deuces Wild, where the proper strategy is to draw to inside straights, break up two pair in some versions, and never discard a deuce, it can be tough to switch to Bonus Poker, where we draw to inside straights only if they include at least three high cards of a jack or better, never break up two pair, and where a single deuce is just another card.

Each video poker game has its own little quirks. You don't want to break up a full house with Aces on top in Jacks or Better just because you're still thinking about the Double Bonus game you just left.

Take a walk. Have a snack. Watch a couple of spins of the roulette wheel. Allow yourself time to "switch gears," then think about your next game of choice.

TIP #80: Don't underestimate low pairs. [JG]

As I walk through casinos, watching other video poker players, one mistake stands out. Most players would improve their game immensely if they showed more respect for low pairs.

In Jacks or Better-based games, too many players toss away low pairs in favor of keeping a single high card. They reason that keeping the high card will bring more frequent payoffs for a pair of Jacks or better. That's true, as far as it goes. You'll get some return a little more frequently if you hold a single high card rather than a small pair.

That leaves out an important part of the equation. The average payback for keeping a low pair is much higher than the average for keeping a high card. Keep a single high card, and nearly 40% of your winners will just return your wager in 1-for-1 paybacks on a pair of Jacks or better. But keep the low pair, and you'll more frequently draw two pair, three of a kind, full houses, and even the odd four of a kind.

The bottom line is not close. In 9-6 Jacks or Better, holding a low pair will bring an average of about 4.1 coins for every 5 coins you bet; hold a single high card, and you get back only about 2.4 coins for every 5 you bet.

Likewise, holding a low pair is a stronger play than holding a four card straight open on either end. You have to get a four-card flush before discarding the pair is to your advantage.

TIP #81: Be on the lookout for straight flush possibilities. [JG]

Often in video poker we'll find ourselves discarding all five cards and hoping for better with a fresh draw. With no pairs, no high cards, no four-card straights or flushes, we're often better off to flush it all.

One proviso: In games such as Jacks or Better or Bonus Poker in which we do not ordinarily hold three-card flushes, we have to be on the lookout for possible straight flushes. It's easy to overlook a hand that includes a 4, 5, and 8 of clubs, not realizing at a glance that a 6 and 7 of clubs would give us a straight flush. The possible 50-for- payoff

95

on a straight flush, combined with other straight and flush possibilities, make this a long shot worth pursuing.

A video poker veteran once told me that friends asked him why they didn't hit more straight flushes. It seemed to them that they hit twice as many royals as garden variety straight flushes. "I watched them play, and found out why." he told me. "They didn't hit more straight flushes because they didn't play for them."

TIP #82: Go for the royals. [JG]

I remember well my first royal flush. My wife Marcy and I were playing in a video poker tournament at the Tropicana in Las Vegas. She was playing in a 20-minute tournament round, and I was passing time at quarter 9-6 Jacks or Better. I held a Jack and King of diamonds—and up popped the 10, Queen, and Ace.

It was rodeo week, and a fellow with a cowboy hat, string tie, Western-style shirt, and jeans and boots caught a glimpse of my screen.

"Now ain't them PURTY," he grinned.

Yes they were. I didn't know it at the time, but they also weren't all that rare. They occur about once every 40,000 to 46,000 hands, depending on the game we're playing and the draw strategy we're using. An average player might play 500 hands per hour. I've been timed at 800, and video poker pros move even faster. We might never see a royal flush playing 20 or 30 hands an hour on the tables, but on the video screens an average player might see one about once per 80 hours of play, and faster players will see them more often than that.

While it doesn't exactly make them commonplace, it makes them attainable, and worth accounting for them in your strategy. We'll even break up some winning hands to go for the big one if we have four parts of a royal. If we start with Ace-King-Queen-jack of hearts, and pair up one of those cards, we break up the pair and go for the royal. If our four big hearts are joined by a 10 of clubs, we break up the straight. If we have one little heart to go with the big ones, we break up the flush.

There's one exception: If we have a pat straight flush consisting of the King-Queen-Jack-10-9 of the same suit, we don't dump the 9 and hope for the Ace. In this case we happily take our straight-flush payoff. Otherwise, it's royalty we're after!

TIP #83: Wide variations in short-term results are normal. [JG]

The house edge at a good video poker game like 9-6 Jacks or Better looks a lot like the house edge at blackjack. Given expert play, in the long run you'll get back 99.5% of everything you wager. That's a 0.5% house edge, roughly the same as a blackjack basic strategy player can expect in a multiple-deck game.

But blackjack players and video poker players take wildly different routes to get to the same point. Blackjack players have many more small winning sessions than video poker players, while video poker players rely on occasional big wins to balance out frequent losses.

Much of the expected long-term payback in video poker is tied to a few rare hands. Royal flushes account for a little more than 2% of your expected long-term payback—the exact figure varying with the game and pay table. That means any video poker game has an exaggerated edge to the house in any session that doesn't include a royal flush.

There will be some winning sessions without a royal. Hit four deuces for 1,000 coins at Deuces Wild, or four Aces for 800 coins at Double Bonus Poker, and you should walk away a winner. Hit a full house or two, or four-of-a-kind or two above the average, and you can have a nice profit at Jacks or Better.

Still, even on games that yield a player edge, the normal expectation is for far more losing sessions than winners. Hit one of the rare hands, and wins can be spectacular!

TIP #84: Slot club cash back makes a difference, so shop around for the best offerings. [JG]

For most slot players, cash back from a casino slot club is a nice little bonus. Recouping a few tenths of a percent of everything wagered can mean some nice pocket money, but it doesn't do much to close the gap between a 95% payback and breaking even.

Video poker is different. Here, it is possible on some machines to close the gap all the way, and even to turn some games into profit opportunities.

One of my regular haunts offers cash back at a rate of 0.25% of your play. Bet $4, and you get a point, and each 100 points can be redeemed for $1.00. So, for every $400 you bet, you get $1 in cash back.

Not only that, but every Tuesday is triple points day. Play on Tuesdays, and you get $3 back for every $400 you bet. The cash back rate becomes 0.75%.

This casino has 9-6 Jacks or Better. Given its 99.5% paypack percentage with expert play, my expected loss is 50 cents for every $100 I bet. For $400 in wagers, my expected loss is $2.

See where this is going? On most days, if I bet $400, I can expect to average a $2 loss, and I'll get back $1 from the slot club. That effectively cuts the house edge in half. And on Tuesdays, my $400 in wagers brings $3 in cash back, not only balancing off my $2 in expected losses, but giving me a $1 profit. The 0.75% cash back from the slot club, added to the 99.5% return on the machine, has turned this into a 100.25% proposition.

There still will be many more losing sessions than winners, but overall the slot club cash back swings the edge in my favor.

This isn't a rare situation. If you're in an area with many casinos, it's worth a comparison shop for the best combination of video poker pay tables, slot club cash back, and multiple-point days.

Part IV:
TIPS FOR OTHER GAMES

Casino managers offer the following gaming options to their patrons for several reasons: The game is so much fun to play that players will risk their money in spite of the odds against them, or the players will try a new game because they've been losing at their favorite games, or the players are so uninformed that they don't know that they have no reasonable chance of winning.

Two other gaming options—"live" poker and sports book betting—are offered because the casinos are more or less guaranteed a profit regardless of the outcome of the games. Players compete against each other, and the house takes a portion of the wager as its fee for offering the gambling opportunity to its customers.

Many of the games that we include in this chapter have been around forever, and occasionally allow the player a fair chance of winning; others have gained popularity within the last few years, and offer limited opportunities for profit. Whatever the case, play the best strategy and your chances of winning will improve.

BIG 6 WHEEL

TIP #85: Don't play this game!! [WT]

Many casinos still offer this game. Players face a vertically-mounted circular wheel containing many numbers, and a betting surface that allows them to bet on the possibility that the number(s) that they wager on will appear on the stop-point on the wheel. Players bet on the numbers, hoping that the wheel will stop on one of them. The dealer spins the wheel, and the winning number is paid off at the odds displayed on the betting surface. Odds generally range from even money to forty-five to one, and the player wins if the wheel stops on a number or symbol selected. All non-matching bets are losers.

Fact is, the chances of beating this game are terrible! The casinos enjoy an "edge" of at least 11% on even-money bets, and as much as 22% on other bets.

BINGO

TIP #86: Play bingo in establishments that offer guaranteed payoffs, regardless of the number of players.

Tip #87: When payoffs are guaranteed, seek out those sessions when there are likely to be less competitors.

Tip #88: Don't play more than two "boards." Your chances of winning don't often merit the increased costs. [WT]

Here's a good example of a game that's very popular, but can be one of the best bets or one of the worst bets! Depends on where, when, and how you play . . .

Gaming revenue reports from Nevada reveal that casinos keep less than 2% of the bingo money that they handle. The game is a "loss leader" and is offered to attract patrons who also play other games that generate higher profits. This is not the case in other gaming jurisdictions, where bingo is a principal source of revenue for the "casino." Profits to management exceed 10% or more of the cost of playing.

Although the game rules—potential ways to win—remain essentially the same wherever the game is played, the number of players in each game and the amount paid to winners decides the difference between good bingo and bad bingo. Good bingo games guarantee payoffs, regardless of the number of participants; good bingo games that offer established payoffs are best played when the number of potential winners is diminished; good bingo games don't require that you play multiple boards in order to substantially improve your chances of winning.

CARIBBEAN STUD

TIP #89: Don't make the one-dollar side bet. The house has a very high "edge" which will whittle away at your bankroll.

Tip #90: Fold every hand that is below ace-king in value.

Tip #91: Bet every hand that contains an ace-king or higher, and a card that matches *the dealer's card*. [FS]

There are two main wagers in Caribbean Stud: the *ante* and the *bet*. The *bet* area looks like a treasure chest bursting with gold coins. The *ante* is the rectangular area. Atop the ante on the layout is the side bet—the jackpot—that is made by dropping a one-dollar chip in the jackpot slot. With this bet, the player becomes eligible to hit the progressive jackpot, or bonus payoffs for the better poker hands.

The rules are simple. Beat the dealer's hand, sort of . . . The player puts a bet in the ante square (and the $1 side bet if he chooses to do so) and the dealer deals him five cards and five cards to himself, with his last card "face up." If the player thinks he will beat the dealer's hand, he must make a bet in the "bet" box that is twice the amount of his ante. If he thinks he can't beat the dealer, he folds, and his ante bet (and side bet) is lost. Once all players have decided to either place a bet or drop out, the dealer exposes his remaining four cards.

Here's the catch: The dealer *must* qualify with an Ace-King for the game to be fully decided. No Ace-King, he only pays the players that placed an ante bet, unless a player made the $1 side bet and has a full house or better. If the dealer has Ace-King or better, then all player's hands are judged against it, and the player's hand wins if it beats the dealer's hand. Antes pay even money, and bets are paid off at house odds.

The truly frustrating part of this game is that the dealer often doesn't qualify, and you don't win the *bet* bonus, regardless of how good your hand is. Playing the best strategy, the casino has a 5.3% advantage on the Ante bet, and a 2.6% advantage on your total action.

KENO

TIP #92: Every keno lounge publishes a list of betting options and payoffs. Shop around for the best odds, for the difference can be many thousands of dollars on a single winning ticket. [WT]

If you enjoy betting on state-sponsored lotteries, you'll like Keno—and the odds are better! It's a simple game. Decide and select which of 20 numbers will be randomly drawn from an 80 number field, bet a buck or so, and win tens of thousands if you guessed right.

The game is both good and bad for the average gambler: It's good because the minimum bet can be a dollar or less, and the number of games played—the number of decisions per hour—is usually less than 10. Compare this to blackjack (with 60 to 150 games per hour and a minimum bet of $5.00) or slot machines and video poker (with 150 to 500 games per hour and a minimum bet of around $1.00 for best-strategy play) and you can see that your exposure to the casino's built-in edge is much less when playing Keno. It's bad because the average house advantage in Keno is 30%! The average player will eventually lose $3.00 of every $10.00 wagered . . . Unless he hits a big payoff and wins thousands!

Combinations of numbers are the key to the game. Nearly every winning combination has odds greater than ten to one, and odds are often in the hundreds or thousands to one. Unlike many other games, the payoffs on winning Keno tickets vary from one casino to another.

TIP #93: Don't select more than eight numbers on a straight ticket. The odds of hitting all 8 are 230,000 to 1—but the odds of hitting all 9 out of 9 numbers are 1.3 *million* to 1! Your best bet (best odds) in keno is to bet *against* one number being selected (3 to 1.) [WT]

Once you find the casino with the most favorable payoffs, decide on a betting strategy and stick to it! The two most common wagers are "straight" bets or "way" bets. With a straight bet you are guessing how many numbers that you select will be included in the 20 numbers selected from the field of 80 numbers. The more correct numbers you select, the higher the payoff.

TIP #94: Bet way tickets rather than straight tickets. The odds are the same, but you'll hit more payoffs. [WT]

A "way" ticket combines multiple straight bets onto a single ticket, at a lower overall cost to the player; it's a good way to spend less per bet while increasing the overall chance of a win. A Keno employee will gladly explain how to make this wager.

Let's dispose of a few myths with a few more tips:

TIP #95: It makes no difference which numbers you select, because each and every number selected in one game has the same chance of being selected (or not) in the next game. Past performance is absolutely no indicator of future performance.

TIP #96: There is no such thing as a winning keno system, in spite of advertisements that offer methods which track and accurately predict which numbers will appear. Save your money, and bet it on keno!

TIP #97: Larger bets don't result in "bonus" payoffs, as is often the case with slots or video poker. Bet small, and savor the possibility of a big payoff from a tiny wager. [WT]

LET IT RIDE

TIP #98: Let your first bet ride if you have a pair of 10's or better, or any three cards to the royal flush. If not, withdraw the #1 bet. Let the #2 bet ride if you made 10's or better and have four cards to a flush. Otherwise, withdraw the #2 bet. [FS]

The object of this game is to obtain a five-card poker hand of "10's or better," with the three cards dealt to you and the two "community" cards dealt to the dealer. Three betting squares, labeled 1, 2 and $, require that the player make a wager in each square prior to the cards being dealt. You are not playing to beat the dealer, as in Caribbean Stud. You receive three cards, must initially place three bets, and have the option to withdraw two of the bets if you don't think that your hand will be a pair of 10's or better. Leave all three bets, and you can win on each bet, or withdraw the first two bets and only lose the last wager if your five-card hand doesn't contain a pair of 10's or better.

What many players don't understand is that you can *withdraw* the #2 bet, even if you let the first bet "ride." Each bet is handled separately and there is a distinct strategy for each bet.

PAI GOW POKER

TIP #99: When playing pai gow poker, learn the best playing strategy, don't make the optional

side bet, and bank as many hands as the casino will allow. [HT]

The objective of Pai Gow Poker is to arrange, or "set" a seven-card hand into a five-card hand and a separate two-card hand and hope that both hands are higher in poker rank than the dealer's corresponding hands.

The rules are quite simple. A single deck of cards is used with the addition of one joker, which can be used as a wild card to complete a straight, flush, or straight flush. Each player makes a bet, and then the casino dealer gives every player, including himself, a seven-card hand with all cards dealt face down. Each player looks at his hand and then sets the cards into a five card "high hand" and a two card "low hand." The five card hand must be higher in poker rank than the two card hand—otherwise, you automatically lose. Once you've set your hands, you place each hand on the layout face-down in the indicated position. The dealer then reveals his cards, and sets his hands (by house rules) into five-card and two-card hands. The dealer then exposes the players' hands and compares them to his hands.

You win your bet if your high hand and low hand are higher in poker rank than the dealer's corresponding hands. When one hand has the same poker rank as the corresponding dealer hand, this is known as a "copy" hand. The banker or casino dealer always wins copy hands. A tie occurs when one hand is higher than the corresponding dealer's hand, but the other hand is lower. When ties occur, no money is exchanged.

The casino earns its money in two ways:

1. From the "natural" banker edge when the casino dealer is the banker.

2. By charging a 5% commission on all winning bets.

The poker ranking in Pai Gow poker ranges from a best hand of five Aces to a worst hand of no pair, just like regular poker, and a basic playing strategy has been developed which explains how to best set your hands—which is beyond the scope of this book. At best, this strategy reduces the casino's advantage to 2.8%.

In most casinos, players can be the Banker in this game; that is, take over the financial advantage enjoyed by the casino dealer. However, if you want to be the banker you must have a sufficient bankroll to bank all bets made by your fellow players. Also, the rules for banking are different from one casino to another, so it's important that you shop around. Your goal is to be able to bank as many hands as the casino will allow.

Some casinos offer an optional side bet for bonus jackpots. The amount of the jackpot depends upon the ranking of the high and low hand. Tempting as it may seem, it's best to avoid the side bet because the casino's edge is too high.

RED DOG

TIP #100: When playing red dog, only make the "raise" wager when the spread is *seven or more*. [HT]

This game is similar to acey-ducey—the game you played as a kid. It's played on a table about the same size as a blackjack table, and all players make a bet before the dealer places two cards—face up—on the layout. Players then have the option to make a second bet (known as the raise wager). The dealer then shows a third card and you win one or both bets if the third card is between the value of the initial two cards.

Even with an optimum betting strategy, the casino's edge is about 3.5%. If the initial two cards are a pair, the dealer will automatically draw a third card, and if it has the same value as the original two cards all players automatically win at 11 to 1 payoff odds. If the original two cards are consecutive (e. g. 4, 5) the dealer will not draw a third card, and the hand is a "push."

Most third card draws occur when there is a "spread" between the original two cards. For example, if the original two cards were 2 and 8, the spread is five—the number of possible cards between 2 and 8 (e. g. 3, 4, 5, 6, 7.) The dealer will announce the spread, and players have the option of making the secondary raise wager (equal to the original bet.) Players win if the third card is *between* the value of the original two cards. The payoffs vary from 1 to 1 up to 5 to 1, based on the spread, but the proper strategy for this game is simple: wait for the "seven or more" spread.

SIC BO

TIP #101: If you are interested in playing sic bo, stick to the "small" or "big" wagers, and only bet every other decision. [AP]

East meets West on the Sic Bo table. Sic Bo has been aimed at the burgeoning Asian market as it is a traditional game from the East, and despite its pretty, luminous layout (a western innovation,) it is an ugly, dull game and anybody who bets serious money at it will be a sick beau indeed!

Sic Bo is truly one of the absolute worst games to ever hit the casino pits. In fact, it's worse than that. It *is* the pits! This game has over thirty different possible bets, only two of which—the *Small* and the *Big*—have a conscionable house edge of 2.8%. The rest of the bets have house edges that range 7.87%, which is awful, to a staggering 47.2%! To top it off, since Sic Bo tables are rarely crowded, the number of decisions in a given hour can be a hundred or more! Remember that a casino makes its money in two ways—the house edge multiplied by the number of decisions per hour. Speed, even in low house-edge games, can damage a bankroll. In high house-edge games, speed can quickly kill a bankroll.

The object of the game, if you're still determined to play it, is to guess which individual die or combination of dice numbers will come up when three dice are shaken. Players make their wagers on a brightly-colored layout that lights up the winning propositions. You can make single-die wagers, two-dice wagers, and three-dice wagers. Here are some of the wagers and payoffs:

Dice Faces: Bet on one number (1 through 6) appearing on one or more dice. This wager is reminiscent of the old Chuck-A-Luck game, and the house edge is 7.87%.

The Two Face: Bet that a given two-face combination will appear on the next shake (for example, 2:4). This wager is paid off at five to one, but the house edge is 16.67%.

The Three Face: Like the Two Face, but you must correctly pick three numbers. The bet is paid off at a whopping 150 to 1, but the true odds of this bet winning are 215 to 1! The house edge is 30%.

Other Wagers: You can also bet *The Couplet, The Triplet,* and *The Totals* wagers, where house edges range from 9.7% to an incredible 47.2%!

Small or Big: You are wagering that the next shake of the dice will result in a three-dice combination that totals from four to ten (Small) or from 11 to 17 (Big). If the dice come up triples—2:2:2 or 3:3:3 for Small, or 4:4;4 or 5:5:5 for Big, the player loses. The house edge is a much more reasonable 2.8%.

THE SPORTS BOOK

TIP #102: Don't bet parlays! [FR]

Betting on sporting events is one of our favorite pastimes. Unfortunately, most bettors don't understand the nature of casino sports betting, the odds they face, or the potential profit that casinos make as a result of their misguided betting decisions.

Let's begin our advice about sports book betting with some basics, and then take a look at "parlays."

Most sports betting wagers involve a "point spread." Since two teams playing each other are seldom equal in ability, the casino, for betting purposes, makes the stronger team "spot" the weaker team some number of points. This brings the contest down to a somewhat even proposition. Now, it's up to you find the stronger side of that bet.

When you bet a single team against the point

spread, you must lay 10% "juice" over and above the amount you hope to win. Thus, if you like the San Francisco 49'ers for $100, you must put up $110 at the sports book counter. If you win, you get back $210, or $100 profit. You are actually laying 11 to 10 odds on your bet, *and that is the sports book's edge.*

Due to these odds, your disadvantage on a single team "straight" bet is 4.5%. That's because for every two bets, you stand to win one for $100 and lose one for $110, putting you $10 behind on $220 risked ($10/$220 = 4.5%.)

Now, *parlays* are a different animal with increased profit appeal. With a basic parlay, you bet two teams instead of one, and they *both* must win or you lose your bet. The upside is, if you pick both winners you get paid 13 to 5 odds! A $100 parlay on two teams will pay $260 in net profit if it wins.

Nevertheless, the parlay is inferior to betting each of the two teams in separate "straight" bets! That's because as attractive as its payoff might seem, your disadvantage on a two-team parlay is 10%!

Here's why: When team "A" plays team "B" and team "C" plays team "D", four different pairs of winners can emerge—A and C, A and D, B and C, and B and D. In your parlay, you will have one of these combinations. Therefore, you have just one basic chance in four of winning your bet. The odds are 3 to 1 against that, but the payoff odds are only 2.6 to 1!

So here's the bottom line: If you bet four parlays for $100 each, you should win one and lose three, putting you $40 behind on $400 risked. Had you made eight straight bets for $50 each instead ($440 worth of action), you should have one four and lost four, putting you just $20 behind. To break even making only straight bets, you need to win 52.4% or your plays. To break even betting two-team parlays, you need to win 52.7% of your plays. What's the obvious conclusion? Don't bet on parlays.

TIP #103: When the point spread on your football pick is between 1.5 and 4 points, bet the money line! [FR]

Here's a simple rule: "Money Line" plays are generally better than straight bets. Although the majority of sports betting wagers involve a point spread, NFL football games are often available two ways: against the "point spread" or against the "money line."

With a money line wager, you're picking your team to win "straight up," with no point spread involved. In effect, you're either *laying* odds on the favorite, or *taking* odds on the underdog. But to give the sports book an edge, the odds you receive on the "dog" aren't quite as high as the odds you must lay if you want the favorite. Here's a clear-cut example:

Suppose the Green Bay Packers are a three point favorite over the Miami Dolphins. With a straight bet, you'd have to lay $110 to $100, and either give or take the three points—depending on which team you picked. We've already established that this gives the house a 4.5% edge, assuming the contest is a 50-50 proposition.

Now, the *money line* on this game would most likely be *"160/140"*. This is known as a standard "20 cent line" (the gap between 160 and 140.) It means that you must lay $160 to win $100 if you pick the Packers to win "straight up," no points.

But you only get $140 to $100 if you take the Dolphins to win outright. Without any edge built in for the house, the true odds for a three point game would be to either lay $150 to $100 with the favorite, or take $150 to $100 with the dog.

Here you can see that the "juice" you're paying is still $10—just as it was with the $100 straight bet—but the money line bet involves between $140 and $160! *After everything washes out, your disadvantage is only 3%!*

The juice on money line bets can be higher or lower than 3%, depending upon the price of the game. The closer a game gets to "pick'em" the closer to the 4.5% the money line juice is. But as soon as there's an established favorite and an underdog, that $10 juice you're giving with the money line is on a larger sum than $100, and the house percentage goes down! In fact, it goes all the way down to about 2.5% just before it shoots back up again!

What do I mean, "shoots back up again"? Somewhere just before the money line odds reach 2 to 1, the sports book's juice gets so low that he builds some extra padding into his prices. A game that has a point spread of "4.5" for example, will often carry a money line of *210/170.* Now the house has a forty cent gap rather than twenty cents, and the house edge is back up to around 4.5%!

TIP #104: Gravitate towards football games on which you can gain an extra one-half point involving a point spread of 3, 4, 6, or 7. [FR]

In football, all points are not created equal! Unlike baseball or basketball, football teams usually score 3 or 7 points at a time. This has a big effect on point spread outcomes.

In the NFL, one game out of every eleven on average finishes with the favorite winning by 3 points *exactly*! In contrast, the favorite wins by exactly 2 points less than 2% of the time. What does that mean to you?

If you're in a position to "shop" for different lines, it will sometimes have a *significant* impact on your team's ability to cover the spread. Suppose for example that most sports books have the 49'ers listed as a three point favorite over the Cowboys. However, down the street another location has that line at 3 and one-half. Normally a one-half point difference in the line isn't a big deal. But because the 3 is the most important point in football, the Cowboys" chance to cover this game has just improved by 4 and one-half percent!

That means if the 3 point line made the game a 50-50 contest, then at 3 and one-half the Cowboys are 54 and one-half percent to cover— and you only need a 52.4% shot to make up for the 11 to 10 juice! Realistically, however, it's hard to find a 3 and a 3 and one-half, or a 2 and one-half and a 3 on the same game. But it's not uncommon to find a 4 and a 4 and one-half, a 6 and a 6 and one-half, or a 7 and a 7 and one-half.

You see, the 3, 4, 6, and 7 are the most common margins of victory in football games. Picking up one-half point on any line surrounding one of these four numbers is *significant*! One of the *least* influential examples in this category would be two lines of 5 and one-half and 6 on the same game. If the 6 was perfect at dividing the contest, then you'd have a 52% shot with the favorite at -5 and one-half. That's not quite enough to cover the juice, but it goes a long way towards making it up.

Of course, deciding which of the two lines is the weaker one is another dilemma that very few handicappers can solve. Nevertheless, if you just pick your team *blind*, then gain a half point involving the 3, 4, 6, or 7, your *average* chance to cover will improve by more than 1%. That alone will cut your built-in 4 and one-half % disadvantage down into the 2% to 2 and one-half % range.

TIP #105: In most instances, betting "middles" is a sucker play. [FR]

Let's talk about "middles." Suppose that downtown at the Horseshoe Sports Book, the Denver Broncos are a 7 and a half point favorite over the Philadelphia Eagles. But up on the Strip at the Mirage, they're a solid +9! Your mouth waters. You can take Denver -7 and one-half Downtown, and get Philly +9 on the Strip for $500 apiece—and the most it can cost you is $50, since you can't possibly lose both bets! But if Denver wins by exactly 8 points, you win both ways and pocket $1,000. Even if they win by 9 points, you win one side and push the other, still netting $500.

That's what's known as a "middle." They sound too good to be true. Usually, they are! In the hypothetical example just given, you're roughly a 30 to 1 underdog to hit the 8 or the 9 (combined) and you're only getting between 10-1 and 20-1 odds on your $50! That would be analogous to accepting 20-1 payoff odds on "snake eyes" at the dice table!

It's not that "middles" are an inherently bad idea. It's just that discrepancies between lines at different sports books seldom leave a wide enough "window" to make betting both sides worthwhile.

What *does* make a middle profitable? Fundamentally, it's no mystery. Since you're getting up to 20-1 on your money, you need at least a 1 in 20 chance to hit your middle. If you could find lines of 2 and one-half and 3 and one-half on the same game, that would do it easily—you'd be getting 20-1 odds on a 10-1 shot! A middle using 6 and one-half and 7 and one-half points would be about a break-even proposition, since you'd be just about a 20-1 underdog to hit the 7 on the nose. Unfortunately, both of the middles are about as rare as hen's teeth. Even very attractive looking middles such as 3 and one-half with 4 and one-half are a long run loser, and so are 5 and one-half with 6 and one-half!

In short, it's hard to find a middle on which your odds against hitting it are shorter than 20 to 1, but a few worthwhile middles would be:

2 with 3	3 with 4	5 &one-half with 7
6 with 7 & one-half	6 & one-half with 8	

Most other available middles nearly always give you the short end of the stick, unless you find some gaping holes surrounding formidable numbers like 9 and one-half with 11 and one-half.

TIP #106: Bet the favorite on the money line, then take the dog plus the points! [FR]

Another way to improve your "win" percentage is to watch for point spread gaps vs. the money line.

When it gets down to playoff time in the pro

119

football season, there are only a few games on the board each weekend. Since these are such high visibility games, sometimes the money line doesn't match up with the point spread, leaving some favorable betting opportunities. This is most common with the Super Bowl game if it doesn't figure to be a close contest.

An excellent example occurred in January 1996 when the Dallas Cowboys were 13 and one-half point favorites over the Pittsburgh Steelers. Normally, a point spread that high should carry a money line of about minus 780/plus 600, since a 13 and one-half point favorite wins the game outright only about one time out of eight. But because it's the Super Bowl, too many bettors would take the Steelers, getting six to one odds. If Pittsburgh should actually win, the sports book would get buried! Hence the game went off at minus 450/ plus 350. This opens a gaping "middle" for alert sports bettors.

Here's what I mean. Suppose you take Pittsburgh +13 and one-half in a straight bet for $260, then lay the $450 to win $100 that Dallas wins outright. Now you've got a 13 point middle that you should be laying 7 or 8 to 1 to get!

What can happen? Four times out of eight, Dallas will cover the 13 and one-half and you'll win $100 on your Dallas money line play, but lose $286 with Pittsburgh plus the points. There you drop $186 net. One other time out of eight Pittsburgh will beat Dallas outright and you'll win $260 on your Pittsburgh straight bet, but lose $450 with your Dallas money line play. That'll cost you $190. The remaining three times Dallas will win, but not cover the points and you'll win both ends for a $360 profit!

Now, if you win $360 three times and lose

around $188 the other five times, you'll get a net profit of $140 overall. That's nearly a 10% player edge rather than a 3 or 4% house edge—*and it's all made possible by the flaky money line price!*

What happened in the Super Bowl back in 1996? Dallas beat Pittsburgh 27-17 and the wise guys looked like geniuses! So keep your eye on the money line prices when they get down to the last couple of playoff games, particularly the Super Bowl. If you can get a 10 point favorite at -330 or less, or a 13 point favorite laying under five to one (or anything proportionally in between): bet the favorite on the moneyline, then take the dog plus the points.

TIP #107: Lean towards underdogs and "bye" teams. [FR]

As a general rule of thumb, Underdogs and "Bye" teams tend to cover. At the end of most seasons in the National football League, more underdogs have covered the spread than favorites. From 1993 through 1998 during the regular season (some 1400 football games) the "dog" covered the number 52 and one-half percent of the time. This does *not* include playoff games, however, since they seem to be a breed of a different ilk.

The modest dominance of underdogs vs. the spread is probably due to the fact that most bettors seem to like the favorites and after all, "What's the big deal about laying 3 and one-half points if you've got the better team?" But the truth of it is, a 3 and one-half point favorite will both win the game *and* fail to cover the spread 13% or 14% of the time! *Winning* and *covering* are two distinctly different things.

Furthermore, if you compare the lines at the beginning of the week with those on Sunday, you'll usually find that many of them have risen one-half point or a point. That's probably because the prevalent "action" on the favorite has pushed those lines a tad higher than they should be. It's rarer to see a point spread come down.

A second minor bias worthy of your observation is that teams just coming off a "bye" week tend to cover a bit more often. Chances are the extra week's rest has provided valuable recuperation time. Since the inception of the "bye" week in 1990 and running through 1998, teams coming off a bye have also covered 52 and one-half percent. An underdog coming back after a bye week could be worthy of *special* attention.

Notice here that merely playing "dogs" and "bye" teams is just enough to cover the 10% juice on straight bets all by itself! It's true that hitting 52 and one-half percent won't make you any money, but the slightly longer end of the stick is an excellent place to begin your search for a winner.

TIP #108: When you and everybody else agree that a line makes no sense, go the other way! [FR]

This may be the most important sports tip of all: You can't out-handicap the linemaker.

When betting professional sports, particularly pro football, *it would be foolish to think you can catch the linemaker in a mistake.* I'm sure that if he wanted to, he could make every game *unbettable* by putting a virtually perfect number on it, which in turn makes the contest 50-50. The thing of it is, *sometimes he has a good reason not to do that.*

The linemaker's main responsibility is to protect the sports books by inducing somewhat balanced action on both sides of a game. When the public's perception of that game is accurate, the linemaker's job is easy—the correct number will indeed split the action and there is no advantageous bet available. I believe most games fall into this category.

But what if, in his infinite wisdom, the linemaker discovers that a particular contest doesn't stack up anywhere near the way Joe Public expects? Suppose for example that the public at large thinks that Miami should be a 3 point favorite at home against Buffalo—but the linemaker finds that due to subtle factors *Buffalo* should actually be favored by 3. Now he has a decision to make.

If he puts the true number (Buffalo -3) on the game, everyone will be all over Miami, and the books will have a 50-50 chance of getting buried! If he puts out the number the public expects (Miami -3,) the game will get even action by everybody except the wiseguys who know what the linemaker knows. If they bet big, the books can get caught with their proverbial pants down. What line would *you* put out?

Let's say they compromise and make the game a *pick* (even)! Now, since Miami still looks like a bargain, *most of the money will be bet on the weaker side!* Miami has in effect become a "trap" play! Haven't you noticed in your years of sports play that when a game looks like a "gimme," it seldom seems to win???

That's why when a line makes no sense, if anything, *you should take the side that looks wrong!*

Here's how to approach this theory rationally. Early in the week if you see a line that looks too low, you should immediately suspect that perhaps it's *not low enough.* Think about it. Why would they put out a number that *really* is too low if *everybody knows* it's too low? As days go by, watch to see if that line rises. If it doesn't, discard the game, concluding that it was just your personal opinion that the line looked wrong. But if the line does rise, it confirms that your opinion matches that of the public, and everybody's pounding the favorite. Now, when it comes to Sunday, take the "dog" with maximum points.

THREE CARD POKER

TIP #109: Mimic the dealer!!! Make the play bet if you hold a queen or higher. [FS]

Mimic dealer.

There, I did it. That was the shortest strategy advice I ever wrote.

Mimic dealer.

I didn't even say mimic *the* dealer, as that extra word would ruin the simplicity of the statement.

Why am I beginning this topic in midstream? Why the truncated language? Why not a standard introduction? Because this new table game is drifting across America, like a seed pod from outer space, and while it looks as familiar as your Uncle Ira, its heart and soul are *not* those of your beloved Uncle—but those of an alien being! (Remember *Invasion of the Body Snatchers,* 1956? "He's my Uncle Ira . . . but he's not my Uncle Ira.)

It's poker, but it's not poker.

When Three Card Poker invades your casino, I want you to know the absolutely best strategy to reduce the house edge and position yourself to win some money from this alien game. All that without verbosity. So . . .

Mimic Dealer.

The objective of Three Card Poker is to beat the dealer's three card hand. There is also an added incentive in attempting to win bonuses for certain premium hands.

This game is quite simple to understand and play. The player can bet three propositions called *Ante, Play,* and the independent *Pair Plus.*

We call the *Pair Plus* wager "independent" because you can bet it without betting on either the *Ante* or *Play.* You don't have to beat the dealer on the Pair Plus wager: Just draw two-of-a-kind or better, and receive an additional payout. Many of these payouts are greater than one to one. For example, three-of-a-kind pays four to one and a strait flush pays five to one.

The *Ante* and *Play* bets are part of the competitive mode between dealer and player. Thus, Three Card Poker has overtones of both blackjack (where the player faces off against the dealer) and noncompetitive games like Let It Ride or slots (where the player does not face off against the dealer.)

The game begins with the dealer giving each player three cards and himself three cards. If he opted to place an *Ante* bet, he looks at his cards and decides to either stay in the game by placing a *Play* bet, or drops out.

Once all players have decided to play or fold, the dealer turns over his three cards. If you beat the dealer's hand, you win the Ante and Play bets at even money. However, the Ante wager pays a bonus for certain premium hands: A strait flush usually pays 40 to 1, three-of-a-kind usually pays 30 to 1, a strait usually pays 6 to 1, and a flush usually pays 4 to 1. The Ante also pays even money for a pair. It is important to note that although both the Ante and Play bets can be lost to a superior dealer hand, the bonus payout for premium hands is *still paid, even on a losing bet.* This is one of the rare times when the casino allows the player to win even when he loses! (Now if that isn't alien, I don't know what is.)

Three Card Poker also has a "dealer qualifying mode" just as Caribbean Stud does. Simply stated, the dealer must have at least a queen high or better. If he doesn't, the players win on the Ante bet and have the Play bet returned to them. Bonus awards are not affected by the dealer qualifying rule. So if the dealer has a queen with any other cards, winning Ante wagers are paid 1 to 1, winning Play wagers are paid 1 to 1, and the Pairs Plus wagers are paid on a bonus schedule.

Like all card games that require choices by players, the strategy you apply determines the extent of the casino's edge over you. The optimum strategy for Three Card Poker when determining whether to place the *Play* bet or give up the *Ante* bet is—one more time for the folks in the bleachers—*mimic dealer!* If you have a queen or better, place the Play bet; if you don't, fold your hand. Any variation from this strategy will increase (sometimes markedly) the house edge over you.

The house has a somewhat moderate edge over you when you mimic the dealer. The Ante and Play hands face a 2.1% house edge, while the Pair Plus bet comes in at a 2.32% edge for the house. The Pair Plus wager has no strategy attached to it as it operates like a slot machine; bet your money, cross your fingers, and hope!

Should you make the *Ante* and *Pair Plus* bet on each hand? A conservative strategy would be to make only the Ante wager, followed by the Play wager when appropriate to do so, and hold off making the Pair Plus wager. A more conservative strategy would be to make only the Pair Plus wager, thus risking only one bet rather than two, and extending your playing time at the table. But if you intend to play the game to its maximum potential, play both the Ante and Pair Plus bets, and the Play bet when you hold a queen or higher.

Since the only playing strategy that will reduce the house edge refers to when you should make the Play bet, you should—you guessed it—mimic dealer.

Part V:
AUTHOR PROFILES

Writers that contributed to this book are world-class experts on the subject of casino gaming. Unlike your Uncle Harry, who taught you to shoot craps, or the guy that you met at a blackjack table in Atlantic City, these people *really* know what they're talking about! It's also interesting to note that every one of them is either a recreational or professional casino gambler; they practice what they preach.

Here's a brief profile on each contributor. Their publications, and how to purchase them, are listed in the Additional Resources section of this book.

JOHN GROCHOWSKI lends his expertise to casino players and the gaming industry alike, through his books, magazine articles, and seminars. He's known as the monthly "Answer Man" in *Midwest Gaming & Travel,* and is a regular contributor to *Chance: The Best of Gaming* and *Chance & Circumstance* magazines. On the industry side, he writes for *Casino Executive, Slot Manager,* and *International Gaming and Wagering Business* magazines.

John is the author of five casino gaming books, and writes a column on gaming for the Chicago Sun-Times. He lives in the Chicago area with his wife and son, and can be reached at PO Box 1488, Elmhurst, IL 60126.

FRED RENZEY is the casino gaming columnist for a Chicagoland newspaper, the *Daily Herald,* as well as a blackjack strategy columnist for *Gulf Coast Casino News* and *Poker Digest Magazine*— but first and foremost Fred Renzey is a blackjack and poker player.

After 30+ years as a professional engineer, Fred retired to do what he does *best*—play, study, and write about blackjack and poker. His critically acclaimed *Blackjack Bluebook* is regarded as one of the most vividly descriptive blackjack books on the market, and his monthly subscription publication, *The Blackjack Mentor Tipsheet,* is responsible for improving the games of hundreds of players across the country.

Fred lives in Illinois, and can be reached by mail at The Blackjack Mentor, P. O. Box 598, Elk Grove Village, IL 60009.

FRANK SCOBLETE is America's number one best-selling casino gaming author, and the editor of a quarterly gaming magazine. After graduating college with two Master's Degrees he spent six years as feature writer, then editor, and finally publisher of a news magazine in Long Island, New York. He free-lanced as a book and restaurant reviewer and also had his own radio program.

In 1975 he decided to try his hand at acting, and eventually co-founded a professional touring troupe, in which he produced, directed, or acted in over 50 plays. While researching the lead role for a play about a down-and-out gambler, Frank went to Atlantic City and became fascinated with casino gambling. He sold his share of the theater company and spent the next six years researching, analyzing, and playing the games. He launched his writing career with articles and short stories for *Win Magazine*, and wrote his first book in 1991. He now has 13 books to his credit plus numerous video and audio tapes, does a weekly radio show, writes for dozens of regional gaming and travel publications, provides consulting services, and still finds time to spend several months a year in Atlantic City and Las Vegas "honing his skills." He now has his own imprint at Bonus Books: "Frank Scoblete's Get The Edge Guides."

Frank lives in New York with his wife, Alene Paone, and his two sons, and can be reached at Paone Press, Box 610, Lynbrook, NY 11563.

ALENE PAONE is the owner and CEO of Paone Press, which specializes in mail-order gaming books and tapes, and of Blue Skies Press, a general publishing house. Her gaming column, "Just Ask A.P." appears in numerous periodicals. She's a frequent contributor to many gaming magazines, and one of the authors of *"The Experts' Guide to Casino Games"* (Carol Publishing Group.)

In addition to writing about gaming, Alene enjoys writing about philosophical and religious issues and has had many articles published in these fields using the name A.P. Scoblete (She's married to gaming writer Frank Scoblete.)

She began her professional life as an actress and stage manager, but changed her career when she and Frank "discovered this whole new world of casinos and casino gambling." She's a successful casino player whose key to winning is simple: "I play the right games, use the right strategies, and apply the right amount of discipline."

Alene can be reached at Paone Press, Box 610, Lynbrook, NY 11563.

HENRY TAMBURIN is one of America's most popular casino gaming writers, and the author of nine best-selling books and video tapes. For over 25 years he's offered advice on how to *intelligently* play the games, through his books, over 600 magazine articles, and over 100 seminars.

Some of his accomplishments include opening the first casino gaming school for players in New Jersey, writing the first weekly casino gaming column in a newspaper, publishing the first newsletter on Atlantic City casino gambling, and teaching the first twelve-week course on casino gambling at a local college. Henry has appeared as a guest on numerous radio and TV programs, and has been featured in many newspaper articles.

He is currently a feature write for *Casino Player Magazine, Chance Magazine*, and many other publications. He also dispenses winning advice for casino players on his popular web site—www.smartgaming.com.

Besides writing and teaching, Henry is an accomplished blackjack player, and has conducted numerous studies to develop winning strategies. He enjoys playing and winning, and enjoys teaching others how to do the same!

Henry received Bachelor of Science and Doctorate degrees in chemistry, and uses his mathematical background to analyze casino games. He lives in North Carolina with his wife Linda, who owns and operates the company that publishes his books and videos.

He can be reached at PO Box 19727, Greensboro, NC 27419, or on the internet at HTamburin@aol.com.

WALTER THOMASON is the author or editor of five casino gaming books including two best-sellers, and writes feature articles and columns for several gaming magazines. He's also hosted and/or been a guest speaker on casino gaming radio shows in Mississippi and Florida.

After completing college and doctoral work, he spent 12 years as a college teacher and administrator. He left this field to start a public auction company, which he's owned and operated for over 20 years.

Walter's principal hobby for the last 30 years has been casino gaming, with an emphasis on blackjack, and his observations while in the casinos prompted him to begin writing about the subject in hopes that his advice would be useful to other players. His best advice is "Do as I say—not as I do!"

His wife, Cynthia Thomason, writes mainstream and historical romance books (five to her credit so far) and his teen-age son, John, is a paid movie reviewer for the Ft. Lauderdale *Sun-Sentinel* newspaper. Writing obviously runs in the family!

Walter can be reached at P.O. Box 550068, Ft. Lauderdale, FL 33355.

Part VI:
ADDITIONAL RESOURCES

The preceding chapter of this book tells you much about the experts that contributed their knowledge to this publication. Our primary motivation in writing this book is to encourage you to go beyond the simplistic information we've presented to you, because the "tips" we've given you—the many "ways" that you can beat the casinos—are only the tip of the iceberg. There is *so much more* that you should know if you wish to be a long-term, successful casino gambler.

If you *really* want to learn the "ins and outs" of casino gaming, you'll have to do much more than learn the basic information included in this book.

The first section of this chapter tells you how to purchase books, video and audio tapes, newsletters, and other gaming publications written by the authors of this book. In most cases their books are available from your local bookseller, or can be ordered and available to you within a few days. Another option is to order direct from the publisher or the author, pay shipping charges, and have the purchase delivered directly to your home address.

Also listed are some book stores and web sites that specialize in casino gaming.

JOHN GROCHOWSKI

John is the author of a series of "Answer Books" that take the reader through playing strategies, odds, history, and fun facts about casino games. All of his books can be ordered from Running Count Press, P.O. Box 1488, Elmhurst, IL 60126, for the listed price, which includes shipping. Autographed copies available upon request.

BOOKS:

The Casino Answer Book (Bonus Books Inc.) is the first of the series of Answer Books. It focuses on blackjack, video poker, and roulette, and covers everything from how an English game called roly-poly led to modern roulette to the right times to double down at the blackjack table. Price: $12.95

The Slot Machine Answer Book (Bonus Books Inc.). John answers nearly 200 questions on slot machines, from their colorful history, with tidbits such as how the bars and fruit symbols wound up on slot reels, to how to best take advantage of modern bonus slots, slot clubs, and tournaments. Price: $12.95.

The Video Poker Answer Book (Bonus Books Inc.) is the third Answer Book. It zeroes in on strategy differences between games, and answers questions like, "How does playing strategy change in Jacks or Better if flushes pay 5-for-1 instead of 6-for-1?" and "What's the difference between Double Bonus Poker and Double Double Bonus Poker?" More than 300 questions are answered, including a chapter of questions submitted by readers on just how video poker games work. Price: $13.95.

Gaming: Cruising the Casinos with Syndicated

Gambling Columnist John Grochowski (Running Count Press) is a compilation of 67 essays on casino gambling, from blackjack to baccarat to slot clubs to progressive betting. Price: $11.95.

FRED RENZEY

Fred's book, and information regarding his "blackjack tip sheet" can be obtained by writing to him at P.O. Box 598, Elk Grove Village, IL 60009.

Blackjack Bluebook (Chicago Spectrum Press) is a highly descriptive manual that illustrates the basic strategy of the game in minute detail, followed be a very enlightening chapter on how to "tweak" your play with borderline hands. It concludes with beginner, intermediate, and advanced level card counting systems. 188 pages. Price: $16.95, shipping included.

FRANK SCOBLETE

Frank's books, audio and video casettes, and quarterly magazine can be purchased by calling 1-800-944-0406.

BOOKS:

Armada Strategies for Spanish 21: How to Sink the Casino's New Game! (Bonus Books: $12.95). Spanish 21 is a game that offers many more exciting options for the players than traditional blackjack. You can double down on any number of cards, split pairs up to four times, win 3 to 2 on blackjack even if the dealer has blackjack, and win special bonuses for "exotic" hands like multiple-card 21s and multiple 7s. To offer such wonderful options, the casino has removed all of the 10-spot cards from the decks (the face cards remain). Traditional blackjack strategies when used against Spanish 21 will result in large house edges and large player losses! But the casinos have not banked on Scoblete's Armada Strategies, which can give the player a monetary edge over the game!

Baccarat Battle Book (Bonus Books: $12.95). The most elegant game in the casino can also be the most deadly for unwary and unwise players. Baccarat and mini-baccarat have some of the lowest house edges of any casino games—yet one is player-friendly and one is player-deadly! Find out which is which, as Frank explains how to reduce your overall economic risk while increasing your fun and your chances to win! If you play baccarat or want to play baccarat, don't go to the casino until you've read this book. Your bankroll will thank you!

Beat the Craps Out of the Casinos: How to Play Craps and Win! (Bonus Books: $9.95). The Captain. Since 1978, he's beaten the casinos at a game that players and critics alike believe is unbeatable. Learn how he does it! This book explains the game and covers the Captain's extraordinary methods of play: the famous 5-Count, the Supersystem, High Rolling without High Risk, and Rhythmic Rolling. You'll be treated to insights that few players have ever had as you follow the Captain and his crew of high rollers as they take on the casinos. This book is the best-selling craps book of all time, and a must for craps lovers and those who want to learn how to play the game to win!

Best Blackjack! (Bonus Books: $14.95). This

book is one of the most enjoyable, intelligent, and comprehensive blackjack books ever written for a general audience! It contains basic strategies for single and multiple-deck games, a simple but powerful card-counting system, and wonderful anecdotes (like the man who walked into Treasure Island with $400 and won $1.4 million!) and insightful analysis. Once you finish reading this book, you will be able to play with an edge over the casino and know how to have fun doing it!

Bold Card Play: Best Strategies for Caribbean Stud, Let It Ride, and Three Card Poker (Bonus Books: $12.95). This is the only book on the market solely devoted to these three games. Learn the best strategies for reducing the house edge against three of the most enjoyable and popular new games. Frank takes you step-by-step through the games, and shows you the best moves to make in all situations—including which hands to play and which to fold, which tables to play and which to avoid, and much much more!

Break the One-Armed Bandits! How to Come Out Ahead When You Play the Slots! (Bonus Books: $9.95). For the first time ever, an inside source reveals where the "loose" and "tight" machines are located. From the birth of the slots in the 1890's to the creation of today's "smart" machines, Scoblete explains how the machines work and how to beat them. You'll learn expert strategies, money-management systems geared to s-t-r-e-t-c-h-i-n-g your time and reducing your risk—everything you need to know to come home a winner.

The Captain's Craps Revolution! (Paone Press: $21.95). This book is designed for serious craps players who want to delve more deeply into the Captain's remarkable methods of play, and includes the Classic and Radical Supersystems, Best Buys, the Oddsman's Bet, "Don't" Strategy, and much, much more!

Forever Craps! (Bonus Books: $12.95). For the first time in print, how to get a real-world edge at the game of craps by combining the Captain's 5-count with the Golden Ruler. Learn how to spot "golden shooters"—those shooters who are changing the odds of the game to favor the player. Learn how to get the most from the casinos' comping systems, and how to successfully compete in craps tournaments. Includes a complete biography of the Captain, as well as exclusive interviews.

Guerrilla Gambling: How to Beat the Casinos at Their Own Games! (Bonus Books: $12.95). Featuring guerrilla techniques for attacking just about every game the casinos offer, this book covers how the games are played, the best short and long-term strategies, and a wealth of additional material and insightful stories.

The Morons of Blackjack (Paone Press: $16.95).

There's more to gambling than just strategies and systems. There's the human side—the side that gets frustrated, angry, or annoyed. This book is an insightful, hilariously funny, but hard-hitting and perceptive look into the human and emotional side of gambling. Scoblete (AKA King Scobe) lets it all hang out in this brilliant book of essays and anecdotes about the games we play and the people we play them with—often to our great annoyance!

Spin Roulette Gold! Secrets of the Wheel (Bonus Books: $14.95). This is the authoritative book for anyone interested in learning how to beat roulette. Frank explains how to get the long and short-term edge over the casinos by discovering and exploiting Biased Wheels and dealer signatures, and describes the Chameleon Strategy to capitalize on lucky players. Contains an analysis of over 10,000 actual spins of roulette wheels with 3,800 spins from one wheel.

Victory at Video Poker! (Bonus Books: $12.95). In addition to strategy tables for over 100 video poker games presented as plain English rules, Scoblete discusses video blackjack, craps, and keno. He also covers the psychology of playing video poker, and whether or not the machines are regulated to give a true game. This is a must read for those starting out in the game.

AUDIO CASSETTE TAPES:

Slot Conquest (Paone Press: $16.95). Frank talks about strategies for breaking today's one-armed bandits. Discover where casinos place the "loose" and "tight" machines, and why. Learn the difference between truth and superstition when it comes to the machines.

Sharpshooter Craps! (Paone Press: $16.95). Frank thoroughly explains the 5-count and how to use it with the various systems developed by the Captain. Contains information on setting and controlling the dice, "darksider" attack methods, and much more! If you understand how the game is played and want to play it to win—this tape is for you!

Power of Positive Playing! (Paone Press: $16.95). An exciting talk about how to beat the casinos at their own games. Frank explains how the casino uses a three-tiered strategy to defeat the players, and he offers a three-part strategy to overcome it. Learn how to get the mental edge!

VIDEO TAPES:

Winning Strategies Blackjack, Winning Strategies Craps, and *Winning Strategies Slots* (Goldhil

141

Home Media: $21.95 Each). Hosted by Academy Award winning actor, James Coburn, these no-nonsense quality video tapes explain the best basic strategies for beating the casino's most popular games.

MAGAZINES:

The NEW Chance & Circumstance (Paone Press: $40.00—One Year Subscription). Edited by Frank Scoblete and published by Alene Paone, this magazine is loaded with content and minus the annoying filler material and casino puff pieces. *C & C* is a full-size, quarterly magazine that takes a no-holds barred look at casinos and casino games: the good, the bad, and the beautiful. The writers have been told to call it as they see it—and, boy, have they! In the past, they have revealed how casinos screw up their own promotions, how to track a roulette wheel and look for dealer signatures, how to get an edge at baccarat, what slots to play and how to play them, what the true odds are for the Megabucks jackpots, how to play expert blackjack and video poker, how to employ the Captain's brilliant methods in craps, and how to get more in comps with less risk. In short, *C & C's* goal is to help you squeeze everything you can from every moment of your casino experience.

The writers for this magazine make up a Who's Who of the best-selling authors and experts: Frank Scoblete, Henry Tamburin, John Robison, Barney Vinson, John Grochowski, Bootlegger, Bob Dancer, Larry Edell, John May, Chris Pawlicki, Don Catlin, Walter Thomason, Catherine Poe, and Alene Paone, to name but a few. You won't want to miss an issue!

HENRY TAMBURIN

All of Dr. Tamburin's books and videos are published by Research Services Unltd., P.O. Box 19727, Greensboro, NC 27419, and can be purchased at the listed price (plus $4.00 shipping) from the above address. Books are also available at retail book stores, Amazon.com, barnesandnoble. com, and at Henry's web site: www.smartgaming. com.

BOOKS:

Blackjack: Take the Money and Run is now in its seventh printing. This book contains beginning, intermediate, and professional level playing and betting strategies that will give you the edge over the casinos. It also contains easy to read basic playing strategy charts, and sections on managing risk, how to disguise your skills, and money management. Price: $11.95

Craps: Take the Money and Run, now in its fifth printing, will help make the game of craps less intimidating to beginners, plus it offers more experienced players a powerful betting strategy based on the multiple-odds bet. Several innovative chapters discuss Hedge Betting, Never Ever Craps, Video Craps, and Tournaments. Price: $11.95

Henry Tamburin on Casino Gambling—The Best of the Best is a collection of 79 published articles by Henry which previously appeared in more than 20 magazines, newsletters, and newspaper columns. The articles are grouped into eight chapters covering the basics of casino gambling, blackjack, craps, slots, video poker, table poker, baccarat, Let It Ride, Caribbean Stud, Three Card Poker, Pai Gow Poker, and Sic Bo. This book tells you just about everything you need to know to play smart and win more. Price: $15.95.

Reference Guide to Casino Gambling—How to Win is a unique one-volume guide covering 25 popular casino games, including the traditional and the new games introduced within the last few years. Tamburin explains the games, the playing rules, the layouts, the odds, the best bets, the casino's edge, and the optimum playing strategies. You will alter your playing habits and win more after reading this book! Price: $11.95.

Winning Baccarat Strategies is a classic, and contains a detailed analysis of baccarat, including baccarat card-counting systems. Price: $19.95.

The Ten Best Casino Bets teaches you which casino games and bets are best for casino players, and how to make these ten best bets. Chapters also cover betting strategies, money management, and the psychology of casino gambling. Price: $3.95.

VIDEOS:

Craps—Deal Me In shows you how to play and improve your chance of winning by watching Henry Tamburin demonstrate and explain how the game is played. You'll learn which bets are best and which to avoid, table etiquette, money management, and a whole lot more! This 90 minute video was filmed in a casino with professional dealers to simulate the real thing. On-screen graphics summarize key points, and a handy index card makes it easy to find any topic. Price: $19.95.

Blackjack—Deal Me In demonstrates and explains how to play blackjack and improve your chance of winning. Dr. Tamburin covers the basic playing rules, proper table etiquette, how to play every hand dealt to you, the importance of money management, and lots more. Segments include hard and soft hands, doubling down, splitting, sur-render, and insurance. A combination of basic strategy charts and review make this an excellent way to learn how to become a skilled blackjack player. This 90 minute video was filmed in a casino with a professional dealer to simulate the real thing. On-screen graphics summarize key points, and a handy index card makes it easy to find any topic. Price: $19.95.

Roulette—Rolling to Win demonstrates and explains how to play roulette in a casino setting with a professional dealer. Tamburin covers the basic playing rules, proper table etiquette, how to make each roulette bet and their odds, the different types of wheels, how to manage your money, and the basics of several betting systems. This 30 minute video has a handy index on the package so you can search forward or backward to any topic. Price: $19.95.

ADDITIONAL ITEM:
Blackjack Strategy Card. This wallet-sized, plastic laminated card contains the complete basic playing strategy. Use it when you play blackjack and you'll always make the correct play! Price: $3.00.

WALTER THOMASON

BOOKS:
Blackjack for the Clueless (Carol Publishing Group): Formerly titled *The Ultimate Blackjack Book*, this book is a guide for novice players, is easy and fun to read, and provides the fundamental

information required to make you a potential winner at this game. Retail Price: $12.00. For home delivery, send $12 plus $4 for shipping to Walter Thomason, P.O. Box 550068, Ft. Lauderdale, FL 33355.

The Experts' Guide to Casino Games (Carol Publishing Group): This comprehensive guide to *all* forms of casino gaming, including sports betting, written by the best-selling authors and players of the games, is unique. Never in the history of casino gaming books have more experts pooled their talents into one publication. Retail Price: $16.95. For home delivery, call 1-800-944-0406.

Twenty-first Century Blackjack: A New Strategy for a New Millennium (Bonus Books): This ground-breaking book presents an alternative to "flat" or "inspirational" betting strategies, or for those who lack the ability, patience, or bankroll required to be successful card counters. Retail Price: $12.95.

For single copies, call 1-800-944-0406. For multiple copies, call 1-800-225-3775.

BOOK STORES

Two of the largest book stores that specialize in casino gaming books are Gambler's Book Shop (1-800-522-1777) and Gambler's General Store (1-800-322-2447) which are both located in Las Vegas. Call and ask them to send you their free catalog. Other outstanding book stores include Gambler's World (Tempe, AZ), Gambler's Warehouse (Biloxi, MS) and Gambler's Book Store (Reno, NV).

WEB SITES

Those of you with internet access can visit any number of web sites that cover the basics of casino gambling. For starters try www.frankscoblete.com, www.suntimes.com (John Grochowski), www.thewizardofodds.com, www.smartgaming.com, www.casinocenter.com, and www.bj21.com.

One final note before we close this chapter . . . A very small percentage of gamblers have problems coping with life as a direct result of their interest in gambling. A national organization, Gamblers Anonymous, can help. If you or someone you know has a problem with gambling, call 1-800-GAMBLER.